Sheila's Mystery

Mrs. Molesworth

In the interest of creating a more extensive selection of rare historical book reprints, we have chosen to reproduce this title even though it may possibly have occasional imperfections such as missing and blurred pages, missing text, poor pictures, markings, dark backgrounds and other reproduction issues beyond our control. Because this work is culturally important, we have made it available as a part of our commitment to protecting, preserving and promoting the world's literature. Thank you for your understanding.

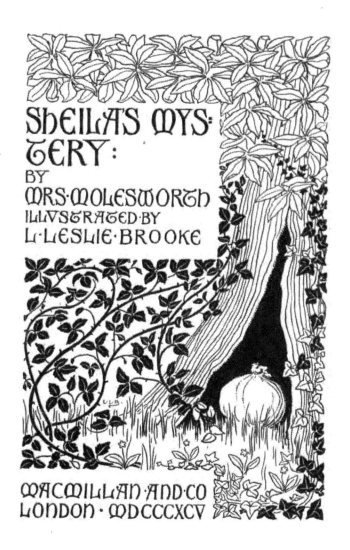

Sheila's Mystery:
BY
MRS. MOLESWORTH
ILLUSTRATED BY
L. LESLIE BROOKE

MACMILLAN AND CO
LONDON · MDCCCXCV

CONTENTS

CHAPTER I
HER OWN ENEMY 1

CHAPTER II
THE HAUNTED WOOD 18

CHAPTER III
GYPSY OR WITCH 35

CHAPTER IV
THE NICE LAME BOY 49

CHAPTER V
AN OPEN WINDOW 66

CHAPTER VI

SHEILA MAKES UP HER MIND . . . 82

CHAPTER VII

IN THE GYPSY CARAVAN . . . 99

CHAPTER VIII

A POOR FRIEND IN NEED . . . 114

CHAPTER IX

LONG AGO 133

CHAPTER X

'YOU ARE NOT LIKE YOUR MOTHER' . . 149

CHAPTER XI

A STRANGER AT CURLEW MOOR . . . 166

CHAPTER XII

CHRISTMAS GUESTS 183

ILLUSTRATIONS

	PAGE
Before either of the others had the least idea what she was going to do, she had darted to the window and flung the pretty case right down among some withered bedding plants	16
For a strange figure was indeed making its way towards the two girls through the trees . .	39
And listen she did, straining every nerve not to lose a syllable	80
Crept stealthily by the other side of the hedge, keeping up with her, though unseen . . .	100
Gathered flowers and tinted autumn leaves for Sheila .	119
'Sheila Josselin,' he repeated. 'Lettice's baby; Lettice's little girl at last'	158
Sheila started as she saw the figures dark against the windows	195

SHEILA'S MYSTERY

CHAPTER I

HER OWN ENEMY

OF the many fortunate children in the world I do not think there could be any with more reason for happiness than little Sheila Josselin. She had everything commonly supposed to be needed for happiness—a very pretty and pleasant home, good health, good ability, parents who loved her dearly, a sister not much younger than herself, who also loved her dearly, and whom, in her heart, she loved too; but yet Sheila was *not* happy.

She seemed to have come into the world with a jarring note in her nature, which spoilt all the sweetness of it, and that jarring note was a jealous, complaining temper. And she did not try as she might have done, as those about her would gladly have helped her to do, to overcome this unfortunate failing. On the contrary, she allowed it to grow, till— but for certain very strange events which I mean to relate in this story — there is no saying what an unlovable and miserable girl she might not have become.

One pleasant day in September, Sheila and Honor came in from their afternoon walk with their governess in time to get ready for the schoolroom tea. For once Sheila was looking cheerful and talking brightly. It was going to be Honor's birthday the next day, and Sheila was feeling happy and excited about the present she had got for her sister.

For she was not a selfish child in a common or greedy way. She would have spent all her money eagerly to please her father or mother or Honor, or any one she loved, but she would have done it *greatly* for her own sake too, though she would have been astonished if any one had said this to her. There was nothing she liked as much as being praised and thanked and admired — as being 'first'—and she was always imagining that people did not love her, or think well of her, or that they were comparing her to her disadvantage with some one else.

Honor was going to be eleven. Sheila was twelve past. The two were not like each other. Sheila was pale and dark-haired—and her hair was neither curly nor wavy—and her eyes, as you can imagine, had rather a sad expression which one does not like to see in a young face. And she had a habit of wrinkling up her forehead as if she had all the troubles of the world on her shoulders, which did not add to her attractions, for already, at only twelve years old, the poor forehead had deep lines across it.

One of Sheila's troubles was that she thought herself very ugly.

It was a mistake, for she had the sort of face which often grows into a beautiful one, but certainly she was not going the way to make it so.

Honor was quite different looking. She was a perfect fairy of sweet, bright, childish loveliness. I rather think her features, if strictly examined, were not as regular and fine as Sheila's, but when you saw her running to you, her hair shining as if the sun was always smiling on it, her dear little face all flushed with pleasure, her blue eyes full of happiness, you could not stop to think about the length of her nose or the shape of her mouth; you just said to yourself, 'What a dear child she is!'

And you would have said rightly. She was a very dear, very good and true, and loving little creature. But for all that there were often, very often, times at which even she *could* not 'get on' with Sheila.

As they sat at the tea-table that evening, both little girls were talking about the birthday that was coming, Miss Burke, their governess, joining in and congratulating herself on the unusually pleasant state of the indoors' weather.

'If it was your *twelfth* birthday, Honor,' said Sheila, ' I could tell you exactly what papa's and mamma's presents would be—at least one or two of them; for I know what they gave me when I was twelve.'

'That was just before I came, was it not?' said Miss Burke, who had not been long with them. 'Now see if I can't guess. Was not one of your presents that beautiful red birthday book with your initials outside—" S. M. J." ? '

Sheila laughed. Miss Burke had guessed rightly.

'What is your middle name?' Miss Burke went on. 'What does " M." stand for?'

'Margaret,' Sheila replied.

'It is a nice name,' said Miss Burke. 'But I do

like "Sheila": it is so uncommon. I don't think I
ever heard it in real life before, though I have seen
it in story-books. And what is your other name,
Honor? Your initials are "S. H. J.," I see? Almost
the same as Sheila's.'

'My name is "Sheila" too,' said the little girl—
'"Sheila Honor," but of course I'm always called
"Honor," because of Sheila.'

'How very funny!' said the young governess. 'I
never heard of two sisters having the same name.'

'It was our great-grandmother's name,' said
Sheila. 'She was a Lady Sheila — something, I
forget her last name—somewhere far up in Scotland.
And it's always been thought a great deal of. She
was very pretty—beautiful.'

'I should have thought it would have been enough
to give her name to the eldest daughter,' said Miss
Burke. 'And you two are *so* different looking.
Nobody would take you for sisters. It doesn't seem
to suit you to have the same name.'

She spoke rather thoughtlessly, for though she had
not been long at Curlew Moor—that was the name of
the Josselins' house—she had been there long enough
to see something of Sheila's unhappy character;
besides which, the little girl's mother had explained

to Miss Burke how anxious and troubled it often made both her and Sheila's father to see this jealous, complaining temper taking such root in the child; and the young governess really wanted to do her good. But Miss Burke herself had a happy, sunny nature, and could not quite understand any one going out of her way to *make* troubles as Sheila did.

Instantly Sheila's pale face grew red.

'I suppose you mean that as I am so ugly and my great-grandmother was beautiful, her name should have been given to Honor instead of me,' she said, in a very cold tone.

Poor Miss Burke! How she wished she had not made that unfortunate remark!

'I don't see how that could very well have been done,' she said, trying to speak lightly, 'seeing that you came first—more than a year before Honor, Sheila. I think it was quite natural to give the name to the eldest—you remember I said so, though I am afraid it was scarcely my place to make any remarks about what your parents liked to do. And as for looks—there are dark beauties as well as fair. Perhaps Lady Sheila was dark, and if so, you may be more like her than Honor.'

Honor was growing nervous too. She was so

afraid Sheila was going to spoil their pleasant evening, as she spoilt so many mornings and middle-of-the-days as well as evenings, by her silly tempers. And in her nervousness the little girl gave her head a shake—it was a habit of hers—tossing back her wavy hair. Just then a bright ray from the setting sun shone in through the window and fell across the pretty 'golden locks,' though Honor did not see it, as she was sitting with her back to the light. But Sheila saw it, and in her rising anger she said some very bitter words.

'You need not shake your hair about like that to show it off,' she said to her sister. 'Everybody knows it's beautiful, and that you're just as pretty as I am ugly. But you needn't put yourself forward like that. There is no fear of my forgetting it, particularly not now Miss Burke is here.'

'Sheila,' said Honor, the tears starting to her eyes, 'don't, *please* don't, you know I wasn't thinking of my hair, and I'm sure Miss Burke didn't mean to vex you. Oh, please don't be vexed, just when it's going to be my birthday to-morrow.'

Miss Burke too looked almost frightened. She had seen outbursts of Sheila's temper a good many times already, but none quite so bad as this seemed likely to be.

'My dear Sheila,' she said, 'do be reasonable. You cannot really think that I meant to call you ugly. Don't you remember my asking if your great-grandmother was dark or fair; and then saying that perhaps you were more like her than Honor?'

'You said that afterwards, when you thought I was getting angry,' said Sheila. 'Of course I know in your heart you think I've got an ugly temper as well as an ugly face, and I don't like people *pretending*, just to smooth me down. If you knew what it was to feel that nobody, nobody in the world, except perhaps——' and she stopped, 'that nobody scarcely, cares for you, you wouldn't wonder at my not being very good-tempered.'

Miss Burke looked grave and sorry, but still Sheila's tone was rather gentler, so she began to hope there was not going to be any violent scene. Honor had left her seat and run round to her sister at the other side of the table, for she was very, very anxious, poor little girl, that the eve of her birthday should not be a stormy one. She threw her arms round Sheila and kissed her.

'We do care for you, we do love you,' she said.

'I love you, you know I do. Was it Honor you meant, poor little Honor, when you were going to say "except" somebody?'

'No,' said Sheila, not very graciously, though she did not push Honor away, 'it wasn't you I was thinking of. It was somebody quite different.' A very pained look came into Honor's blue eyes.

'I know who it was,' she said. 'It was Mildred Frost.'

Sheila did not answer.

'It isn't good of you at all to say that,' Honor went on. 'She isn't a sister to you; she isn't even much of a friend. You haven't known her more than a few weeks, and——'

'Yes I have,' said Sheila. 'I knew her first two years ago.'

'Well, that was only for a little while, when she was staying here just as she is now. I don't like her, she is not a true sort of friend,' said Honor.

'You have no right to say that,' answered Sheila. 'She cares for me and she understands me, I know that.'

'Honor,' said Miss Burke, 'come back to your seat and go on with your tea. I think you are both getting into a very useless discussion. You should not be prejudiced, Honor. If Mildred Frost is a friend of Sheila's, you should try to like her. She is the tall girl who comes to the dancing class with the Willoughbys, is she not?'

'Yes,' said Sheila, 'she is their cousin, and she is the only great friend I have ever had. I wish she lived here always. She's going away very soon, but of course she is coming to Honor's birthday party to-morrow, with her cousins.'

'I wish she wasn't,' said Honor. 'It will quite spoil it if she does the way she did when we went to the Willoughby's last week. She got Sheila into a corner and wouldn't talk to any one else, and she is very fond of secrets and mysteries. Janie Willoughby doesn't care for her, and Jack says she's very affected.'

'My dear Honor,' said Miss Burke, rather surprised, for it was not like kind little Honor to speak against any one, 'I don't think Miss Frost's cousins should talk of her in that way, and I don't think you should listen if they do.'

Honor grew rather red.

'I didn't mean to be unkind,' she said, 'but I don't like her.'

'Well, you are not going to see much more of her,' said Miss Burke, 'so I don't think she need be

the cause of any trouble between you and Sheila.
And it will be easy for Sheila to prevent her behaving sillily to-morrow.'

Sheila looked rather pleased at this. She always liked to be made of importance.

'It is only that Mildred is very fond of me,' she said. 'I don't want to spoil Honor's birthday.'

So, for the time, peace was restored. And Miss Burke felt rather glad that Mildred Frost had been mentioned, as the discussion about her with Honor had distracted Sheila's attention from her own fancied grievances.

But, alas! to a character like Sheila's causes of offence are never long wanting. The birthday was not many hours old before her temper was again aroused, and unhappy and gloomy thoughts took the place of the bright and kindly ones with which she awoke.

This was how the new trouble came.

Sheila had for long been preparing a birthday present for Honor. She had taken no one into her confidence about it except Miss Burke, who had been bound over to keep the secret most carefully. The present was an embroidered handkerchief-case, and Sheila had taken the greatest pains with it, for she was not naturally very neat-handed or skilful, and of course she had only been able to work at it at odd times. She had given up many a half-hour which she might have spent in reading some of her favourite story-books, for Sheila was a great reader, and Miss Burke had really admired her unselfishness and devotion.

You can therefore imagine how startled the young governess felt when on the birthday morning, while she was still in her own room, there came a tap at the door, and Honor, brimful of delight, burst in.

'O Miss Burke, dear,' she said, 'I *had* to come to show you my lovely presents from papa and mamma. They were at the foot of my bed—that is what mamma does always; she puts them there after we are asleep the night before our birthdays. Do look!' and with great glee she displayed what she called 'a ducky little umbrella'—Mr. Josselin's gift; and—after the umbrella had been duly admired —a really lovely handkerchief-case, made of rich silk, with the initials 'S. H. J.' exquisitely embroidered in the centre.

'Isn't it *splendid?* Did you *ever* see anything so beautiful?' said Honor, a little surprised at Miss Burke's silence.

'Indeed it is, *most* beautiful,' she replied. 'But, Honor, dear,' and she hesitated. What could she say? If only she had known about it before, she would have tried, somehow or other, to get Mrs. Josselin to change the present, even though her promise to Sheila would have made it impossible to give her full reasons for asking this. Now, she much feared it would be too late. But still— 'Honor, dear,' she repeated, 'could you trust me enough to—not to show your mother's "sachet" to Sheila, or to speak of it to her till—you will understand what I mean as soon as you see *her* present?'

Honor looked puzzled and a little distressed. She was a simple-natured child, not as quick as Sheila in taking up a meaning, and perhaps rather matter-of-fact.

'I'll do anything you think I should, dear Miss Burke,' she said, 'though I can't understand, and Sheila is sure to ask where mamma's present is. What can I say to her?'

'I will try to see your mamma at once,' said Miss Burke, 'and she will tell you what to say. Don't you think if I asked Meddowes'—Meddowes was Mrs. Josselin's maid—'to tell her that I want to see her very particularly for a moment, that she could manage it? Mrs. Josselin must be nearly dressed. She is always early,' and Miss Burke went on hurriedly fastening her dress with nervously trembling fingers.

'I'll run and look for Meddowes,' began Honor, and she turned to leave the room, when a tap at the door was immediately followed by the entrance of Sheila, a parcel done up in tissue paper in her hands, an unusually bright and smiling expression on her face.

A sharp pang of regret went through the young governess's kind heart as she caught sight of the little girl—but, alas, it was too late!

'I couldn't help running after you when Rachel told me where you'd gone,' she said. 'You don't mind, do you, Miss Burke? Here's *my* present, Honor. It's been a secret from everybody except Miss Burke, and I——'

But before she could say more her eyes fell on the magnificent 'sachet' lying on a chair.

'Oh!' thought Miss Burke, '*why* didn't I throw something over it!'

'What is that?' said Sheila, in a strange voice, growing very red, and pointing to the chair.

Honor did not hear her. She was busily engaged

in unwrapping Sheila's present, most carefully done up in ever so many papers, and tied with silver cord. Miss Burke, really not knowing what to say, turned away and began moving about the trifles on the dressing-table as if looking for something.

Then Honor, though by this time she had quite taken in the meaning of Miss Burke's mysterious hints, burst out eagerly, hoping by her hearty and affectionate thanks to soften Sheila's disappointment.

'Oh, Sheila, darling, *how* lovely! You don't mean to say you made it yourself for me? *How* good of you, and just think how rich I shall be in sachets. I shall keep this one for regular use, and mamma's will come in when I am older. I do think it is *rather* too grand for a little girl, and then this one is your very own work, *dear* Sheila.'

She chattered on, though any one who knew her could have seen she was nervous. But Sheila stood like a statue, and when Honor pressed up to her, throwing her arms round her neck to kiss her, the elder girl drew back almost roughly.

'Was it *mamma* who gave you that gorgeous "sachet"?' she said, in a hard dry voice, which poor Honor knew as well as weather-wise sailors know the first warning rustle of the storm-wind among the sails and cordage.

'Yes, I said it was mamma's present,' replied Honor, trying to talk as if there were nothing the matter. 'You see, of course, she didn't know you had thought of the same, and you both knew I wanted a handkerchief-case very much. But it doesn't matter the very least. I am delighted to have them both: they are as different as they can be, and I can use——'

'*Mine* for common, for everyday rough use. Yes, exactly. It is all it is worth, I know, and it is really *most* kind of you to condescend to accept it. But I think I have a little voice in the matter,' said Sheila, and she snatched it out of her sister's hand.

The window was open, Miss Burke had just pushed it open more widely—the garden below was wet, for it had been raining in the night, and the soil in the beds was damp and sticky. Before either of the others had the least idea what she was going to do, Sheila had darted to the window and flung the pretty case, which had taken her so many, many hours of patient toil, right down among some withered bedding-out plants, left there too long by the gardeners, all spoilt and soiled by the heavy showers which had beaten them down to the earth. There it lay—the prettiest side turned to the dirty soil—its freshness and delicacy already gone.

'If you try to fetch it, or to clean it, or any nonsense,' said Sheila fiercely, 'I will run down before you and trample it into the ground with my own feet.'

Then she turned and left the room, turning back for one moment at the door to say—

'It was a plot and a trick. I see it quite plainly. To think *mamma* should have done it! I suppose she will say it was to teach me self-control. She hates me, I know, and so do you, you little pretending humbug, and so does everybody.'

Then she banged the door behind her.

CHAPTER II

THE HAUNTED WOOD

Miss Burke and Honor looked at each other. Both their faces were white. The young governess had never seen Sheila *quite* so wild with temper before. Then Honor burst into uncontrollable sobbing.

'O Sheila, Sheila,' she cried, 'and to think it's my birthday!'

Miss Burke was very sorry for her, very, very sorry. The gentle little girl did not deserve such treatment.

'My dearest child,' she said, 'do try to be calm. Think how all this will distress poor Mrs. Josselin. You must believe that poor Sheila does not mean what she says; that she does not know what she says. For the time she is really the slave of her own jealous, miserable temper.'

Honor tried to check herself. She got out her handkerchief and rubbed at her eyes.

'But, Miss Burke,' she said, 'it's getting worse. Every time she says unkinder things. What can I do? And it makes papa and mamma so unhappy when we quarrel.'

'It cannot be called a quarrel this time,' said the governess. 'I must tell your mamma all about it myself. But, Honor, darling, the bell for prayers will be ringing immediately. See here, bathe your eyes a little and try to look more like yourself.'

Honor obeyed, but as she passed the window her eyes fell on the spot where the unfortunate sachet had alighted.

'I will run down at once and see if it is much spoilt,' said Miss Burke, noticing the child's glance, for she was farther back in the room and could not see out so far.

But Honor turned and shook her head.

'Look down, Miss Burke,' she said, 'it's *gone*. Sheila has been there herself already. I shouldn't wonder, no, I shouldn't wonder if by this time she has burnt it.'

Sheila did not appear at prayers. And poor Mrs. Josselin's loving birthday greeting to Honor was clouded by anxiety as to what the new trouble could be. Miss Burke explained all that had happened, and a stern message was sent up to Sheila, who had shut herself into her own room, by her father, desiring her to come downstairs at once, and that he would stand no nonsense. She dared not disobey, but you can imagine that the little party round the breakfast-table was gloomy and constrained, though every one except Sheila did their best, for poor little Honor's sake, to seem as bright and cheerful as usual.

Sheila sat in silence, her forehead wrinkled in a hundred lines, looking like a miserable, sour-tempered, little old woman. She dared not push away the breakfast that was put before her, but she scarcely ate anything. Altogether she seemed so wretched and unlovable that, in spite of her indignation with the child for the needless unhappiness she was causing, Mrs. Josselin's heart ached for her.

It would be painful and useless to dwell upon Sheila's feelings and behaviour through that unfortunate birthday. After breakfast she was shut up with her father and mother for some time in the library, and spoken to strongly and earnestly, though most kindly. But it was no use. She had 'hardened her heart'; she was holding its door open to all kinds of unlovely guests; and as she stood there in moody silence, her father almost felt that he would have done better to leave her to herself.

And, unluckily, a few words of his at the very last, when his patience was really exhausted—for even the very best of papas and mammas *are* only faulty human beings!—undid any good impression that, unknown to herself perhaps, his plain, wise, gentle words had begun to make.

'If this sort of thing occurs again, Sheila,' he said, 'and of course your own sense tells you that it was peculiarly aggravated by this being poor little Honor's birthday—if *nothing*, no consideration for others, or indeed for yourself, will teach you to control that detestable, jealous, suspicious temper of yours, then I give you fair warning that I won't stand it. I will not have my house upset by the presence of a girl who makes every one in it as unhappy as she *can*. I must find somewhere else for you.'

Sheila did not speak. She was just leaving the room, but something made her look up at her father as he said the last words, with a curious kind of inquiry—a strange sort of threatening.

'You do not love me,' she said; 'you never have loved me. That is at the root of it all.'

Mrs. Josselin caught the expression in Sheila's

eyes, and as soon as the door was closed she turned to her husband.

'Arthur,' she began, 'I wish you had not said that. Sheila, whatever her faults are, is not a shallow character. I could imagine her doing—oh, I don't know what—if she were driven desperate.'

Mr. Josselin gave a little laugh.

'My dear Evelyn, you are fanciful,' he said. 'Perhaps I should not have said that about sending her away—but really, she needs bringing to her senses.'

Mrs. Josselin was silent. Then she spoke again hesitatingly.

'You don't think it possible that—no, we have been so careful. But still the fear of any mistaken impression is always over me. I shall be so glad when it is all clear and above-board about——'

'So shall I,' interrupted her husband. 'It has always been a worrying position to me. But still—*so far*, Evelyn, up to now, and considering that child's extraordinarily perverse nature, I think we may be glad that we were bound down as we were. It would have been *worse* otherwise—she would have imagined real grounds for all this jealousy and suspicion.'

'Poor child!' said Mrs. Josselin, with a sigh.

There was only one streak of light in Sheila's unhappy heart that day, and it came from a very misleading and unreliable source. The idea burst upon her as she left her father and mother.

'I will tell it all to Mildred this afternoon,' she thought suddenly. '*She* cares for me and will sympathise with me. How glad I am she is coming. I do hope it will be a fine afternoon, so that we can be out-of-doors a good deal. It would be so much easier to get her to myself for a talk in the garden than in the house.'

This plan made her exert herself a little to do away with the traces of the morning's disturbance. It was a whole holiday; she did not need to be more with Honor and Miss Burke than she chose; and though Honor tapped at her door two or three times, begging her to come to the conservatory to choose the flowers for the tea-table, or to give her opinion about the games they should play, trying to invent some little reason for getting Sheila to join her as usual, she was always answered by a quiet 'No thank you. I would rather be alone.'

But the tone did not sound so gruff or surly as at breakfast-time, the once or twice Sheila had then been obliged to speak, and Honor, who was always hopeful, went back to Miss Burke in better spirits.

'She's getting round again, I do think,' was her last report. 'Poor Sheila, we must try to seem just as usual, mustn't we, Miss Burke? It must be so uncomfortable for her. And I do believe it's going to be a beautiful day. Perhaps after all we shall have a happy afternoon.'

Things really did look more promising by luncheon-time — the children's dinner-hour. The day had turned out quite lovely; the sun was as bright and warm as if it had been July instead of late September: there was no doubt that the expected guests would enjoy outdoor amusements more than anything else.

'Up to tea-time, that is to say,' said Mrs. Josselin; 'it would not do to have tea in the garden, I fear, for there has been so much rain that the ground must be damp still. So after tea you can amuse yourselves in the house.'

'That will do beautifully,' said Honor. 'Playing out-of-doors first will take down our spirits a little, and then quieter games will do in the house. You know there are three or four boys coming, mamma? The two Willoughbys, and little Malcolm Harley, and the lame boy who has come to live at The

Wilderness. He *is* such a nice boy, isn't he, Miss Burke? We saw him at the Harleys', when we went there to play lawn tennis.'

So she chattered, more to take away the still remaining constraint than because she had anything special to say. And Mr. Josselin, as well as his wife, felt grateful to the little girl for her unselfish good-humour.

Sheila was quiet, very quiet, but she had changed her dress for the better one she was supposed to wear on Sundays and holidays, which was a good sign. Her hair was neat, and the traces of tears on her face had almost disappeared, and she was perfectly submissive and polite in manner.

'Poor dear,' thought her mother. 'I do hope she is making up her mind to be reasonable. Even if she cannot bring herself to say how sorry she is, we must let her see we are more than ready to meet her half-way.'

She would have felt less hopeful had she been able to read what was passing in Sheila's mind; how all her thoughts were absorbed in planning how she could arrange to have a good long private talk with her friend and confidante—Mildred Frost.

Now Mildred Frost was more a silly girl than a

naughty one. She had been badly brought up, or one might almost say not brought up at all. For she had no mother, and the aunt who kept her father's house was quite old and knew very little about children. Mildred had been allowed to read anything that came in her way, and her head was full of romances and exciting stories of mysteries and thrilling adventures. She was not a clever girl, though she thought herself so; she had not sense enough to distinguish between what was true to life and what was not. Her cousins, the Willoughbys, did not care for her much; the girls were younger than she, simple, hearty children, who thought her very clever, and were rather afraid of her, while the boys voted her 'affected' and conceited. She had found her visit rather dull, though her uncle and aunt were very kind, till she met the Josselins at the dancing-class. She immediately made great friends with Sheila, partly, I am afraid, because, as Mr. Josselin's elder daughter, Mildred thought her new acquaintance must be a person of consequence, and partly because she was the nearest to herself in age of all the little party; for Mildred was fourteen.

Mrs. Josselin scarcely knew how intimate Sheila had become with this girl, and I daresay she would

not have minded if she had known it, for she was
very fond of Mrs. Willoughby, and naturally took for
granted that her niece was nice and sensible. Sheila
had at first no idea of hiding anything about her new
friend, for she was by nature candid and truthful.
But by degrees, as Mildred led her on to talk more
and more about her home troubles and how unkindly
she was treated, and how Honor was 'put before her'
in everything, and how nobody really understood or
loved her, Sheila began to say less about Mildred at
home. Her honesty of character made her feel a sort
of shame at remembering how much she had spoken
against her own nearest and dearest to this girl who
was almost a stranger.

Yet there was a kind of fascination about it which
she could not resist. Mildred flattered her, and she
was really, though most unwisely, sympathising. She
thought Sheila very interesting, with her pale face
and black hair and delicate features; above all, her
melancholy dark eyes. She was quite Mildred's idea
of a heroine of romance. And all sorts of fancies
crowded into the girl's silly little head when Sheila
recounted the long story of her woes.

On the birthday afternoon, the Willoughbys and
their cousin were the first to arrive. They were

warmly welcomed, and Honor at once ran off with the brothers and sisters to choose the best ground for some of their favourite games, leaving Sheila and Mildred on the lawn. This was just what Sheila wanted.

'Mildred,' she said eagerly, 'I must have a talk with you. How can we manage it? The other children will be arriving directly, and I shall have to help to entertain them.'

'We must manage it somehow,' answered Mildred, looking very important. 'Wait till they have all come, then we might join in one or two games at first and slip away quietly when they are all busy and would not notice. Is there anything new, dear? You *do* look so white and worn.'

'Oh, I am so miserable, so perfectly wretched!' said Sheila. 'This morning I really felt desperate. If you had been nearer, I think I should have run off to you, Mildred. The worst of it is that this time it was *mamma* who hurt me so. Mildred, none of them care for me. What is the real reason?'

'You must tell me all about it when we can have our talk, darling,' said Mildred. 'You do not know how much I think of you. You are always in my thoughts. It is really very mysterious. But hush!'

and she put her fingers on her lips, 'there are the children back again, and I see the Harleys and that lame boy coming up the drive.'

Very soon all the guests, in number about sixteen, had assembled, and for some minutes there was a pleasant little bustle of greetings and talking, and several pretty presents were given to Honor, who thanked her friends with her usual bright heartiness.

'A photograph of baby, and in such a lovely frame!' she exclaimed, as she undid Joan Harley's parcel and held up the picture of Joan's little brother of two, a sweet cherub of a boy, and a great pet of Honor's; 'and the very books I have been longing for from Mrs. Kelford—and, and—oh! what a dear gypsy doll for my grotto!'

This last was from Conan Sherwood, the lame boy, and the only child of a widow lady who had lately taken a small house on the Harleys' grounds known as 'The Wilderness.'

Conan's face lighted up with pleasure.

'Mother dressed her,' he said. 'You know you told me the other day you wanted an old woman for your grotto, and we thought a gypsy with a red cloak would look nice. And do you know,' he went on eagerly, 'there are some real gypsies on the common? We passed them coming here.'

'Yes,' said Malcolm, 'they came yesterday. And father says they are real gypsies, not those common van people. They've pitched tents quite properly, and father says if they behave properly they need not be disturbed. Father knows about them, you see, with being a magistrate.'

This was very interesting, for it is not very often nowadays that 'real' gypsies, as the boys called them, are to be met with, and all the children stood listening eagerly, even including the very grown-up young lady of the party, Miss Mildred Frost.

'I have never seen a gypsy,' she said. 'They never come where I live. It is too large and bustling a town. They always come to out-of-the-way places, don't they? Oh dear!' she went on, without waiting for an answer, 'how I should like to have my fortune told!'

'I don't think mamma would let us do that,' said Joan, the eldest of her cousins.

'Not *you*, perhaps, you're only a child,' said Mildred. 'But it's quite different for me. I know a lot about gypsies, though I've never seen any. I have

read about them. They have wonderful occult
power. They can discover secrets that baffle every
one else.'

No one knew exactly what 'occult power' meant—
by this time the children were by themselves—so
every one listened respectfully, and Mildred looked
round her with satisfaction.

'I should be very frightened to have my fortune
told or anything like that,' said Joan. 'Suppose
all sorts of very sad things were prophesied. I
don't think it can be meant for us to do such
things.'

'No,' said Honor, 'I shouldn't like it at all. But
now, do let us fix about the games. Shall we divide
into two parties, as we often do, and have two
leaders, and take turn about for choosing the games?
Let me see—will you be a leader, Sheila dear, and
you, Mildred?'

But both declined, Mildred declaring she knew
nothing about games, and Sheila giving no particular reason, the truth being that the ugly imp
Jealousy was again busy at her ear, whispering that,
birthday or no birthday, a younger sister like Honor
should not put herself so forward, 'queening it over
you,' as Mildred expressed it, when the pair of friends

at last found themselves alone for their confidential talk.

For their indifference had ended by irritating the others.

'If they don't want to play, leave them alone,' said the boys, and in the end, though with great reluctance on Honor's part, his advice was taken.

Sheila and Mildred turned off in the direction of a little copse at the back of the house.

'It's a beautiful place for talking in, with no fear of being overheard,' said Sheila. 'It's a little chilly there though, for the sunshine is kept out by the trees. You are sure you are warm enough?'

'Oh yes,' said Mildred, adding, as they came to the stile over which they had to climb to get into the wood, 'it does look dark and mysterious. Do you often wander here alone, my poor Sheila, when things are pressing hard upon you and you long for sympathy?'

'No,' said Sheila bluntly, 'I don't. The trees wouldn't give me much sympathy, would they? Besides, it's rather *too* lonely. I'm not sure that I should like to come here quite by myself.'

Mildred stood still and looked about her.

'Is it haunted, or—or anything like that?' she said hesitatingly.

'Oh no, I don't suppose it is,' said Sheila. 'There's some old story of a witch that made herself a hut here, hundreds of years ago, and no one dared turn her out till she died. She used to wear a red cloak, and she could catch the rabbits with her hands, and everybody was very frightened of her. I wonder she wasn't burnt to death in those days. Of course it mayn't be true. It's only what the people about, say. This isn't our own home, you know. We've only lived here ten years or so.'

'Oh!' said Mildred, 'I didn't know that. Then do you remember your own home? Do you remember when Honor was born?'

'No, of course I don't remember when Honor was born. She's only a year and a month younger than I. How could I? And I *scarcely* remember where we lived before. I'm not quite sure. I think I do a very little. Why do you ask such funny questions, Mildred? I want to tell you about my unhappiness to-day, not to waste time about nonsense. I want——'

But, to her surprise, instead of listening, Mildred suddenly clutched her arm tightly.

'Sheila,' she said in a whisper, and she really grew quite pale, 'this wood *is* haunted. Don't let us stay here. I'm sure I saw *something red* a moment ago, passing behind those trees—over there, where it's a little clearer.'

CHAPTER III

GYPSY OR WITCH

THE two girls stared at each other for a moment or two. Then Mildred tremblingly turned her eyes again in the direction she had pointed out.

'No, there's nothing there now,' she said, 'but I'm *sure* I saw something.'

'It must have been your fancy,' said Sheila. 'I had no idea you were so fanciful. It was just because I was telling you about the old witch who dressed in red. Very likely all you saw was a tiny glint of sun creeping in through the branches. Lots of the leaves are beginning to look a little red now.'

For Sheila had plenty of good sense where her own touchy temper was not concerned.

Mildred was not convinced. But Sheila would not agree to leave the wood. They need not go far into it, she said, but it was by far the best and quietest place for talking in. And Mildred was rather subdued by her fright, so she gave in to the stronger will, and Sheila proceeded with her confidences, almost crying again when she related how she had 'worked and slaved' at the present for her sister, which she chose to consider had been so scorned.

'*Perhaps*,' she ended up, '*perhaps* it was wrong of me to say mamma had done it on purpose. I was in such a rage. But—I could *see* Honor didn't care for my sachet; all she said was in a sort of put-on way, to smooth me down. They don't care for me, Mildred, that's the secret of it all. I am a perfect alien in my own home. Nobody loves me, except you.'

'It does look like it,' said Mildred. 'It is very strange.'

Then Sheila went on to relate the talk of the day before about her ancestress, Lady Sheila, and how Miss Burke had 'as usual' put 'Honor before her.'

Mildred listened attentively.

'It is very odd altogether,' she said. 'And you and Honor are so unlike each other. Can there be any mystery? Supposing—just supposing, Sheila, you were really not their child, and that that was why they care for Honor so much more than for you.'

She spoke half thoughtlessly, half from her intense
relish for anything that savoured of a romance. But
she had not calculated on the effect of her words.
Sheila grew deadly white—her very lips seemed
white, and she half fell back on the trunk of a tree
behind her.

'Mildred,' she said, her voice sounding quite
strange and hoarse, 'have you any reason for what
you have just said? Have you heard anything of
that kind hinted?'

Mildred felt frightened at the effect of her words.

'Oh no, of course not. Don't look so dreadfully
startled, Sheila. I shall be afraid to say anything if
you take it up so. But if it is really true that your
father and mother and Honor don't care for you,
there must be some reason for it, you see. I was
only thinking what it *could* be.'

'And you have heard nothing—nothing at all?
It is only your own idea?' persisted Sheila.

Mildred hesitated.

'Well,' she allowed, 'I have often heard people
remark on you and Honor being so unlike each
other. Anybody would notice it. But then neither
of you is particularly like Mr. or Mrs. Josselin.
Honor has a little look of your father perhaps; they

are both fair. And, if anything, you are more like your mamma, though she hasn't nearly such dark hair and eyes. I once——' but she stopped again.

'You once what?' said Sheila impatiently. 'You had better tell me everything.'

'I once heard some lady ask Aunt Willoughby if you and Honor were whole sisters—not half-sisters, I mean,' said Mildred, 'because you were so unlike each other.'

'And what did she say?' asked Sheila, her tone almost fierce.

'She just said "Oh yes," at least she had never heard to the contrary, or something like that.'

'And what did the lady say?'

Mildred began to get impatient.

'Sheila, I wish you wouldn't question me so. I can't quite remember. I have a confused idea that she repeated some gossip she had once heard about an old Mr. Josselin having adopted a child. But it couldn't have been your father. She said "*old*," I'm sure, and it was far away—not here at all. Still it stayed in my mind, I suppose, and made me notice when I got to know you well, dearest Sheila, how unlike you two were. And—it *is* so strange that you are treated so and not cared for.'

For a strange figure was indeed making its way towards the two girls through the trees.—p. 39.

Sheila did not answer. She was thinking deeply. Then she suddenly spoke.

'Mildred,' she said, 'you will always be my friend. I can always count upon you, can I not?'

'Always, darling. Count me your truest friend. But—you won't tell any one what I have said to you? You *made* me, you know.'

'*Of course* not,' said Sheila. 'You seem to think I have no sense of honour. Besides—whom could I tell? I am alone, utterly alone in my own home. If I were a boy, I——'

But she stopped, startled by her friend a second time clutching her tightly by the arm.

'There it is again,' she whispered in a terrified voice. 'I knew I was not mistaken. O Sheila— it is the witch : the witch's ghost, I mean; and she —oh, what shall we do ?—she is coming towards us.'

There was some excuse for her terror, and for half a moment Sheila was half inclined to turn and fly, in cowardly fashion. If it would have been any good to fly from a ghost ! For a strange figure, bent and huddled together with age, was indeed making its way towards the two girls through the trees—a figure covered up in a red cloak—head and all—just as the old witch had been described.

But a second glance somewhat reassured Sheila: the red figure was no ghost. It came on, crunching the crisp soil under its feet in a very earthly way, and now and then coughing a little as if to catch their attention.

'Don't be silly, Mildred,' said Sheila, catching hold, in her turn, of her friend so as to prevent her running away. 'It's not the witch. It's—a gypsy—a real old gypsy, don't you see? She must be one of those from the camp on the common.'

Mildred ventured at this to look again. But her fears were not altogether dispelled even now. She was, in fact, as many silly, boastful people are, very cowardly.

'Are you going to speak to her?' she said. 'Do you think you need? And after all she may have something to do with that dreadful old witch. I do feel so terrified still, Sheila.'

'It's much safer to speak to her,' said Sheila, though I think curiosity was her real motive. 'Gypsies are very easily offended, and, you see, I am in my own home here. They have very strong ideas about hospitality. If she thought I was rude, she might——'

'What?' whispered Mildred, in a shaking voice.

'Who knows? Turn us into rabbits or root us where we stand, so that we couldn't get out of the wood till she chose,' said Sheila.

She was in a curious, half-reckless mood. She enjoyed teasing Mildred, and yet through all she was very miserable. Mildred's thoughtless words seemed to have given shape to her own distorted fancies. She almost felt like Saul when he fell back appalled at the result of his own presumption—as if the jealousy and morbid complaining she had nourished were going to turn into some real and terrible fact.

Now putting aside all exaggeration and superstition, everybody—'wise' everybodies, I mean—knows that gypsies are strange beings. They may have powers that ordinary folk very seldom or but in small measure possess—powers of reading signs and portents invisible or meaningless to others. We cannot say. But it is certain that they are gifted with extraordinarily quick perceptions and instincts—they really seem able to tell what one is thinking about, and it is difficult to deceive them. And besides this, they have wonderfully good memories and great skill in putting two and two together. Odds and ends of family histories, of local gossip that they come across in their wanderings, are stored up in their minds, like the old-fashioned housewife's hoards, which are sure to come in handy even after seven years; and, unlike the old housewife, who often forgets what her hoards consist of, they seem able to put their finger on the very thing wanted, at once.

I am speaking just now of real, true gypsies of the thoroughbred kind. And these are rare and growing rarer, though people often confuse them with the many wandering dwellers in vans, and haunters of fairs, some of whom have now and then a little gypsy blood in them, though they are very different from the strange mysterious race that for many centuries has haunted Europe.

But the gypsy who was now coming through the trees to the two girls was a real one—a true 'Romany.' She was very old; not improbably she was older than you would find it easy to believe, yet she was still wonderfully strong. Bent as she was, she would have thought nothing of walking at a stretch a distance that many even of you young folk would think twice of attempting; summer's sun and winter's cold, however extreme, only seemed to toughen her wiry old frame, and out of her brown face, wizened and dried up almost like that of a mummy, gleamed two brilliant black eyes which gave a very queer sensation indeed to any one she chose to fix them on.

And though they did not know it till she was pretty close to them, these same eyes had been taking very sharp account of both Sheila and Mildred while she was still at some distance. She knew the characters she had to deal with.

'Good-day to you, my ladies,' she said, with a smile which had something almost condescending in it. 'A fine day for the time of year and a pleasant wood to stroll about in.'

Mildred's *ghostly* fears had vanished, but she still looked and felt frightened. She had never met a real gypsy before—outside of her romances, that is to say—and she felt as if the strange black eyes mesmerised her.

Sheila, on the contrary, reared her proud little head and looked the old woman straight in the face —for once appearing the bright, brave maiden, nature meant her to be, though her eyelids still bore some traces of her tears.

'Good-day to you,' she replied. 'Do you want anything here? This is our wood, you know. It is private. Are you going to the house?'

Mildred gave Sheila's arm an invisible squeeze.

'Don't make her angry,' she whispered very low; but the gypsy heard the words.

She smiled again, this time more scornfully. But the scorn was for Mildred, not Sheila.

'No place is private from old Diana if thither her feet would bear her,' she said. 'But I am not going farther. My business to-day is here. You would like your fortune told, even though you tremble, missy?' and she turned to Mildred, and before the girl knew what she was about, the old woman had seized her hand.

Mildred tried to draw it away.

'Oh no, no!' she said, 'I'm far too frightened, and I haven't any money in my pocket.'

'I wouldn't take it if you had,' said the gypsy. 'You have none to spare—I am not a beggar. And I have not much to tell you,' but she kept firm hold of Mildred's plump, rosy hand, which seemed huge in comparison with her own tiny brown fingers. 'You are going a journey—soon—yes, to-morrow.'

'To-morrow, or the day after, I'm not quite sure which,' said Mildred, meek with surprise and awe.

'To-morrow, I say,' repeated the gypsy. 'And at its end a dark stout man will meet you, a man with spectacles.'

'Oh dear!' said Mildred; 'yes, that's papa.'

'He is a good man,' said the gypsy, 'but he is not a wise father. However, time will teach you; you are only a child and will never be much more. A fair man with brown eyes will come some day, and you will learn better as a wife than as a daughter. But beware of meddling with what does not concern you,' and she suddenly raised her head and gazed warningly into Mildred's face, red with excitement and annoyance and importance, all mixed together. And then she let the girl's hand drop as sharply as she had taken it up.

'Come away, Mildred,' said Sheila. 'You will be satisfied, now you have had your fortune told. I don't want to hear any more nonsense,' and she took her friend's arm and turned to go, thinking to herself that it would be as well to give the servants a hint of the visitor about the place.

But she had reckoned without her host. Old Diana planted herself right in front, and, as the path was narrow, Sheila could not have pushed past her without rudeness, which would have been the greater to so aged a woman.

'No, no, my little lady,' said the gypsy, in quite a different tone from the one she had used to Mildred,

'I have not done with you yet. And you are a lady born. You would show respect to one who might be your great-grandmother, and more than that; above all, as you are in your own home, or at least what you think——' but here she stopped abruptly and peered up into Sheila's face. 'You have been weeping since the sun rose this morning,' she said. 'Those eyes have shed tears to-day and will shed them again ere he sets. Come, cross my hand with silver. From such as you, Diana will not scorn it. And who knows what she may have to tell you?—ways out of your troubles you little dream of; a future such as many a princess might envy.'

Sheila laughed, but there was a touch of nervousness in her laugh which the old woman was quick to perceive.

'I don't mind crossing your hand, as you call it,' she said, and from a little purse she happened to have in her pocket she drew out half a crown, 'but I don't want my fortune told. Only one thing: You must finish your sentence about my being in my own home, or thinking—thinking what?'

The gypsy laughed. This was just what she had wanted.

'Give me your hand,' she said, and in spite of her determination, Sheila no longer refused.

'Ah!' said Diana, with some muttered words of satisfaction. 'I thought so,' she went on, looking up after a moment. 'I knew it; you have troubles before you, my child. Those very near you will cause you more tears and bitterer than you have yet shed. Things are not what they seem. But——' and here she seemed honestly puzzled, and vexed with herself for being so. 'Cross my hand again,' she said, and this time a bright new shilling followed the half-crown. 'No matter, all will right itself in the end. Keep up heart. The future is clear. You will find your true place, and when that time comes, think of old Diana.'

She let go of Sheila's fingers. But Sheila was not to be so easily dealt with as Mildred.

'No,' she said angrily, 'you must tell me a great deal more. Why am I not in my true place? You do know what you mean, and you shall tell me. Do you mean that I am not myself—not Sheila Josselin? Who am I, then, and why do papa and mamma not love me as much as they love my sister?'

'*Sister!*' repeated the gypsy. There was a world of hints and mystery in her voice. But Sheila was not treating her the right way; she was so little accustomed to keep her temper at any time that it was not to be much wondered at that she lost it now.

'Yes, *sister!*' she said, almost stamping her foot. 'You are an impertinent old cheat, to say such things. I shall tell papa, and he will send the police or somebody after you. I—I won't——' but just then a terrified tug from Mildred made her look round. 'What are you doing, Mildred?' she said. 'I will say what I choose, and——'

'She's gone!' cried Mildred. 'I *am* so glad!' And —yes, as Sheila looked round again she saw it was true. Already the red cloak was some yards off, and as they watched it, it disappeared, almost as if its owner had sunk into the ground. 'Sheila, Sheila!' Mildred went on, 'she *is* the witch after all, I do believe.'

'Nonsense,' said Sheila, 'there she is again. She had only hidden behind a tree for a moment, to frighten us, I do believe. How can she get along so quickly? An old thing like that! She had no right to go off without explaining what she meant by her hints. I wonder if it would be any use running after her.' And she stood for a moment uncertain, as if half inclined to start.

CHAPTER IV

THE NICE LAME BOY

BUT Mildred caught hold of her.

'Oh no, no! Do let her go!' she entreated. 'I have never been so frightened in my life. Besides, you wouldn't get anything more out of her, Sheila. You shouldn't have got angry with her. They won't be bullied. I know that much about gypsies and witches and those kind of people, whether you laugh at me for being frightened or not.'

There was truth in what Mildred said, and Sheila felt rather ashamed of having got into such a temper.

'I wish I hadn't got angry,' she said. 'I do wonder what she meant.'

'I'm afraid you will never know—not from her, at least,' said Mildred. 'It *is* very queer. If ever you do find out anything, Sheila, you'll be sure to write and tell me all about it, won't you? Promise me you will.'

'Of course I would,' said Sheila, 'but—I don't think there *can* really be any mystery,' and she gave a little shiver. 'It doesn't seem as if it *could* be. But I do wish you weren't going away so soon, dearest Mildred. Are you sure you won't stay a little longer?'

Mildred shook her head.

'Quite sure,' she said. 'I am going home to-morrow or the day after—there will be a letter fixing it by the second post to-day. And now, I am sure it will be to-morrow. You heard what the gypsy said. Wasn't it queer about the "fair man with brown eyes," Sheila? It isn't often that fair people have brown eyes, you see. I wonder if I have ever seen him already. I shall always remember about it.'

'Yes,' said Sheila, 'it was rather strange. But you see they always talk that sort of way. I think what she said to me *much* queerer. Mildred, I can *always* count upon you, can't I? I do need a true friend.'

'Always, darling,' said Mildred. 'Write *everything* to me. I will count your letters sacred. If only I lived nearer you! I would do anything in the world for you.'

'Even if I were poor and lonely and could do nothing for you in return?' said Sheila wistfully.

'Of course, dearest. You don't suppose I love you because you are rich and have a pretty house and things like that?' said Mildred.

And in a sense she meant what she said.

But, all the same, Sheila's words startled her just a little. She had no wish to get herself into any trouble for her friend's sake.

'Perhaps,' she thought, 'it's rather a good thing I am going away, for Aunt Willoughby and Mrs. Josselin might be angry if they knew all Sheila has told me. And she has got such a temper that one can never feel sure what she mightn't say if she was angry. They might put all the blame on me of her fancies, if they *are* fancies.'

Sheila squeezed Mildred's arm fondly.

'It is a comfort to have *one* friend,' she said. 'You must give me your address. It is Hexford, isn't it? But I don't know the name of the house. Is it far from Hexford?'

Mildred grew rather red. The truth was, her father was not at all rich, and her home was only a small house in the middle of the little town where he practised as a lawyer. Her mother, Mrs. Willoughby's half-sister, had been of better birth than her husband, and Mildred was fond of talking as if she herself was really a person of no small importance.

'Hexford is enough,' she said. 'Papa is so well known. Our house hasn't got a proper name. I believe it was once called "The Pollards," but papa thought it was a silly name.'

'I think it's rather nice,' said Sheila. 'Have you a lot of pollard elms? How long does it take you in the railway to Hexford?'

'Only about three hours. We change at Wraylington Junction,' said Mildred quickly. She was anxious to avoid answering about the 'lot of elms.' 'It is rather tiresome sometimes having to wait for the trains there; if they don't—— But, Sheila,' she broke off abruptly, 'don't you hear some one calling you? I am sure I do.'

Sheila stood still to listen.

Yes, there came a cry—

'Sheila, Sheila, She—la!'

Mildred looked rather startled.

'I hope we haven't stayed too long,' she said. 'I shouldn't like Mrs. Josselin to be vexed with me.'

Sheila turned round on her impatiently.

'You are really too cowardly, Mildred,' she said. '*I* don't care, and if I don't, why should you?—the last time we shall see each other for so long. What does it matter if they are vexed or not? They don't care for me or love me, and if you are my friend you should stand by me.'

Mildred tried to smooth her down. But to tell the truth, she was beginning to think that the position of being Miss Josselin's bosom friend and confidante had its drawbacks.

Then again sounded the voice, nearer this time.

'It is some one coming to fetch us,' said Mildred.

'Very likely,' replied Sheila coolly.

And so it was. Another moment or two brought them in view of Conan Sherwood, the lame boy, who was stumping along with his crutch valiantly in their direction.

'Fancy sending *him*, poor boy,' said Sheila, on the lookout to blame somebody. 'O Con,' she called, when he was within hearing, 'have you been hunting for us? I am so sorry. I hope you're not tired.'

'Oh no!' said the boy cheerfully. And, indeed, it was seldom that Conan was anything but cheerful. 'Walking doesn't tire me now a bit, since I've got so much better; only, you see, I can't *run*. So I offered to come and hunt you up. They've all been wondering what's become of you, and—I'm afraid Mrs. Josselin isn't quite pleased. She came out a little while ago and asked where you were.'

Sheila tossed her head.

'It's very good of you, Con,' she said, 'but really it doesn't matter. It would be something *quite* new for mamma or papa—or anybody—to be pleased with me.'

And out of a sort of perversity she walked on as slowly as possible. Mildred looked uneasy; Conan distressed. He was very fond of Sheila, though he had not known her long, for one of her best qualities was real tenderness and sympathy for any one suffering or feeble.

'Do let us hurry,' said Mildred at last.

'Con cannot go so fast,' said Sheila.

'Oh yes, I can! Or if you would run on, I'd come after you slowly,' he said. 'I would have found you sooner, but I had an adventure on the way. I met one of the gypsies from the common—*such* a queer old thing!'

'Did she stop you?' asked Sheila with some curiosity.

'Yes,' replied the boy, laughing. 'She offered to tell my fortune, but I said I hadn't time to wait. She *would* keep me a minute or two, though. She was rather amiable. She told me life had not been all roses for me, which I knew already, but that I had a great deal to be thankful for, which I know still better. I don't suppose there's a fellow in the world who's got a jollier mother than I have, and that's the best thing there can be, isn't it?'

'Was that all she told you?' asked Sheila.

'N—no; she said something rather queer—that I should beware of meddling with what didn't concern me. I nearly laughed, for I thought perhaps I was doing that already. But won't you walk a little faster, Sheila?'

'Oh, *please* do,' said Mildred, 'for my sake, Sheila. It would be rather horrid, really, for me to get into a scrape the very last day of my visit. And very likely aunt would think it was all my fault.'

They had not very far to go now, so Sheila consented to hurry a little, Conan following at his own pace. But the girls were already too late to escape a rather sharp reprimand, and I must say not an undeserved one, from Sheila's mother.

'Where have you been and what have you been

doing, Sheila?' she said. 'I cannot blame Mildred, for I have no doubt she only went to please you. But how could you be so selfish and unkind as to separate from the others—spoiling poor little Honor's pleasure on her birthday so?'

Perhaps it would have been better if Mrs. Josselin had said nothing till they were alone. But she was really vexed, for she could not bear any discourtesy to be shown to the young guests. And she was sadly disappointed, too, for she had been hoping that the unhappiness of the morning was to have a good ending after all, and that Sheila was really humble and anxious to make amends, though her proud spirit would not allow her to say so.

And now all these hopes were again shattered.

Sheila said nothing, but almost any words would have been better than the look on her face and the half-smile of something very like contempt with which she turned away.

'Sheila,' said her mother, 'do you not hear me?'

The others had made their way across the lawn, with Honor and Miss Burke, to the house, where tea was now ready. Mildred felt extremely uncomfortable.

'I'm—I'm so sorry, Mrs. Josselin,' she began.

'I'm afraid it was partly, or a good deal, my fault. I suppose I wanted to have Sheila to myself, and I didn't think much about any one else. For this is the last time we shall see each other.'

Mrs. Josselin felt rather surprised. As I said, she had not realised the tremendous friendship that had sprung up between Sheila and this girl, whom she looked upon almost as a stranger. Indeed, she had seen so little of Mildred that now, for the first time, it struck her how different she was from her cousins, the Willoughbys. The tone of her voice, something in her accent and manner, startled Mrs. Josselin a little. There was a decided want of refinement, and something more—a want of perfect straightforward candour; a touch of cringingness.

'Have I done right—have I been careless?' thought Sheila's mother, with a little pang. 'Can it possibly be this girl's influence that has made the child so much more unloving and strange-tempered of late? How unfortunate if it is so, just when I was hoping so much from Miss Burke's bright, healthy character.'

And the tone in which she replied to Mildred was so cold that the girl felt herself rather 'snubbed,' which did not, on the other hand, make her feel more amiable to Sheila. For though she had blamed herself in speaking to Mrs. Josselin, which was a 'way' of Mildred's, in her heart she did not think it at all her fault.

'It is quite different in your case,' Mrs. Josselin said to her, 'and I should not think it right to reprove you. *Sheila* is hostess here, and she owes attention and kindness to all her guests equally.'

They were standing alone on the lawn, the others having by this time reached the house. To Mrs. Josselin's surprise and almost terror, Sheila turned round fiercely.

'I am *not* hostess here. Honor is put before me in everything. I am treated as if I were a dog, and it is difficult to believe I belong to you at all, mamma, when I see the difference made between her and me. I will say it for once, even before a stranger, as you choose to treat my best friend, Mildred. *She* cares for me and she knows how I am treated. For the first time in my life I have found some one to love me, and so, of course, you are cold and unkind to her.'

Sheila's face looked almost ghastly, she had grown so pale. Her mother was terribly shocked; and as for Mildred, she was shaking with fear and vexation. This was not at all what she had been counting upon as the result of her friendship with Mr. Josselin's elder daughter! There was certainly now no chance of her being invited to stay at Curlew Moor, and she felt thoroughly angry with Sheila.

'O Sheila!' she exclaimed, 'you shouldn't speak like that. Indeed, indeed,' she went on, turning to Mrs. Josselin, 'I haven't made mischief as you might think. I know Sheila is very often unhappy, and I was sorry for her. I am often unhappy at home myself. I have no mother, and——'

Here she began to cry.

'Sheila *has* a mother. That makes all the difference,' said Mrs. Josselin quietly. 'I do not blame you, Mildred, as much as Sheila, though I do think you are old enough to know how very seldom the repeating over home troubles does good, and how very often it does harm. But as you and she are not likely to see much more of each other in the future, you need not distress yourself about all this. I trust that Sheila will soon feel sorry for the wild things she has said, and I regret that what should have been a happy day for all concerned has been so spoilt.'

'So do I, I'm sure. I'm dreadfully sorry,' said Mildred, drying her eyes.

She followed Mrs. Josselin meekly enough to the house, and did her best to hide from the others that anything was the matter. So that, on the whole, when Sheila's mother said good-bye to her that evening, she had come to think rather better of the girl, and spoke to her kindly.

'She is silly, and rather common,' she thought. 'But then, poor girl, she has no mother. Though, after all, when I see how terribly I have failed with poor Sheila, I can scarcely feel as if my own child were much the better for having a mother!'

And poor Mrs. Josselin's heart was very sore.

Sheila remained standing alone on the lawn. Neither by word or gesture had her mother invited her to accompany Mildred and herself to the house. For almost the first time, Sheila began to be a little frightened at what she had done. Had she at last gone too far? What would be the result?

'Perhaps,' she said to herself, 'they really will send me away to school or somewhere. Well, after all, I don't know that I should care much if they did. Anything would be better than going on living like

this, and feeling every day more and more certain
that they don't care for me.'

A footstep coming towards her made her turn
round. It was Conan. Poor Conan, no one had
thanked him much for his good-nature, and yet his
only wish had been to prevent any troubles he could.

'Have they all gone in?' he asked breathlessly,
as he got up to Sheila. 'Then you weren't very late
after all. I do hope Mrs. Josselin wasn't vexed.
Were you waiting for me? How kind of you.'

Sheila felt rather ashamed.

'To tell you the truth, Con,' she said, 'I had forgotten about you. It was a great shame, for it was
very kind of you to come to fetch us. But—mamma
has been very vexed with me, more vexed than ever
in her life, I think. She has gone into the house
with Mildred, and left me here.'

'I'm so sorry,' said the boy. 'But hadn't we
better go after them now, Sheila?'

'*You* had,' said Sheila, 'but I can't. I daresay
mamma would order me out of the room if I went
in. Never mind about me,' she went on, seeing how
shocked and distressed the boy looked; 'you can't
understand it all. Your mother loves you and you
love her. It's quite different. I'm used to it.'

But Conan was too kind to take her at her word.

'Oh, do come in!' he said. 'Mrs. Josselin can't be so vexed as all that. You haven't done anything so very naughty. Do come, Sheila. You can't stay out here all the evening by yourself.'

Sheila yielded so far that she began walking towards the house.

'I'll come in,' she said, 'but I really can't go into the dining-room. They're all at tea there. You go in, Con, and if mamma wants me she'll send for me. And if she doesn't, never mind. I'm pretty well used to staying alone in my own room. Some day I expect I'll——' she stopped.

'What?' said Con. Then, as she did not answer, he looked up anxiously in her face. 'Sheila,' he said, 'did you see the gypsy? Did she speak to you? I hope you didn't let her talk any nonsense to you. Mother says it isn't right to try to tell fortunes: we are not meant to know the future. Were you going to say some day you'd run away, or something like that?'

Sheila began to laugh. But there was not much mirth in her laugh.

'What an absurd boy you are, Con!' she said.

'*Girls* don't run away. Where could I go to? I didn't want to speak to the gypsy. She would speak to us. But that has nothing to do with it. I had been unhappy all the morning. I'm pretty nearly always unhappy, and so would any one be who had my life.'

Con did not know what more to say. He had known a great deal of trouble in his short life, but not *this* kind of trouble. And it made him very sorry indeed.

Sheila was softened by his distressed face; for, as I said, all the best of her came out to any one who touched her pity, like this sensitive, delicate boy. If by a lucky chance her mother had happened to send for her, if Honor had come running with some kind little word of coaxing, as many and many a time had been the case when Sheila deserved it as little as now, all might have been well—all at least might have turned out very differently. But the mother's patience was, for the time at any rate, exhausted, and Honor dared not do anything, seeing how really displeased Mrs. Josselin was.

When Con went into the dining-room, Honor jumped up eagerly.

'O Con,' she said, 'we were just going to look

for you, and then Miss Burke saw you coming across the lawn with Sheila. Where is she?'

'I—I don't know,' said the boy, afraid of making matters worse by anything he said. 'I think she's gone upstairs to her own room.'

Honor slipped round the table to Mrs. Josselin, who was pouring out tea at one end.

'Mamma,' she whispered, '*mayn't* I run upstairs to fetch poor Sheila? I won't be a moment, and—you know, mamma dear, it's my birthday.'

Mrs. Josselin hesitated. Her first inclination was to say 'No—no,' very decidedly, but a glance at Honor's wistful face and at Con's anxious one—for the boy had followed her round the table—made her waver.

'She does not deserve it,' she said in a low voice. 'But still—well, yes, dear, you may go. Don't be long.'

Honor was off like a shot, while Mrs. Josselin made room for Conan beside herself and began talking cheerfully as she went on with her duties.

The little queen of the day meanwhile had rushed off upstairs to Sheila's room. The door was fastened on the inside, so she knocked, at first softly, then a little more loudly, but without getting any answer. Then she called through the keyhole.

'Sheila, Sheila dear,' she said, 'it's me, Honor. Do let me in, Sheila dear.'

But there was no answer.

Honor grew uneasy. Her mother had said she must be quick. It was very unkind of Sheila not to let her in.

Suddenly an idea struck her. There was another door into Sheila's room—a door not often used except by the housemaids, as it opened into a back passage.

'She will not have thought of locking it too,' said the little girl to herself, and in another moment she had run round to it. Yes; the handle turned—it was open, and in she hurried.

But only to be met by disappointment. There was no Sheila there!

CHAPTER V

AN OPEN WINDOW

The fact was, that Sheila had not been in her room at all that afternoon. She had locked the door in the morning and had left it so on purpose, making her way out by the other door, as she did not want Honor or Miss Burke or any one to come to her room in their usual friendly fashion. But it gave poor little Honor a start to see that she was not there.

She unbolted the door and came out on to the front passage, wondering where she could look, and if she dared stay away any longer. And just then she caught sight of Ellen, Mrs. Josselin's old nurse, who still took care of the little girls to some extent.

'O Miss Honor, my dear,' she said, 'if you're looking for Miss Sheila, you may spare yourself the trouble. She ran in to the nursery a few minutes ago and asked me to send her some tea down to the little study; she's in one of her tempers, I'm afraid. Leastways she will be if she's meddled with; so best leave her.'

'O nurse,' said Honor, 'I came to fetch her. Don't you think she'd come?'

Ellen shook her head.

'I'm sure she wouldn't. She said as much to me just now,' said the old woman, laying her hand on the child's arm. 'Leave her to herself for once, my dear. She's been too much gone after and coaxed when she's got into those naughty humours, and it's going too far for anything.'

So Honor, with a sigh of disappointment, felt that she must give in, especially as she had so promised to be quick. She made her way back to the dining-room, only whispering to Mrs. Josselin as she passed her chair—

'She wasn't in her own room. Nurse says she is in the little study, but she thought it was no use.'

'Better not,' Mrs. Josselin said in reply. 'It may be a lesson. Now try to be cheerful, dear.'

And for her sake, and the sake of all her young guests, Honor did her best. Her kind little heart was aching, but no one would have guessed how sorely. And she had her reward, for an hour or two later, when all the visitors said good-bye, every one of them repeated that the afternoon had been a very happy one.

Only Mildred Frost did not seem to recover her usual spirits.

'Please tell Sheila I think it was *too* bad of her to behave so,' she said to Honor. 'Tell her she might have come in and been nice for my sake, especially after getting me into such a scrape as she did.'

Honor's fair face flushed.

'I don't know anything about Sheila getting you into a scrape as you say,' she replied rather hotly. 'You are older than she. And if she wouldn't come in to have tea with us all for *my* sake, on my birthday, I don't think it is likely she would do it for any one else's.'

Her voice trembled, and for a moment it almost seemed as if she were going to cry. But she had been practising a good deal of self-control all day, and another effort was not much to make. So she choked back the tears. She did not like Mildred, and she did not want her to think that she and Sheila were not happy together, as sisters should be.

'Well, anyway you can say good-bye to her for me, as I am going away to-morrow,' said Mildred.

'Very well, I won't forget,' said Honor. 'I'm afraid poor Sheila's head is aching. I'm going to sit with her now.'

She couldn't help feeling in one way glad when they had all gone, though a few tears dropped at the thought that her birthday was really over—the birthday she had looked forward to so much and so long.

'Rude, stuck-up little thing,' thought Mildred to herself, as she was driving home with her Willoughby cousins. 'I can't bear Honor Josselin,' she said aloud. 'I wonder any of you like her. I think she is so conceited and affected.'

The Willoughby children, as I have said, were a little in awe of Mildred. They were younger than she, and had had some experience of her ways behind the scenes, though on the whole she was good-natured and amusing to them.

'She's always *very* nice to us,' said Joan, the elder girl, 'and she's much sweeter-tempered than Sheila.'

'Oh!' said Mildred, with a laugh, 'I grant you Sheila has got a perfectly horrible temper. I can't understand any one taking the trouble to be so cross as she makes herself. Still, I like her better than Honor. There's nothing sneaking about her.'

'*Honor's* not sneaking,' said Jack, who was Joan's twin; 'she's about the unsneakingest——'

Mildred put her hands up to her ears in pretended horror.

'Oh, spare me, Jack, for goodness sake!' she said. 'I had no intention of bringing a storm of defence about me, I assure you.'

'Then you shouldn't abuse people who've just been being very kind to you,' said Jack sturdily.

'I wonder if Uncle Willoughby pays extra for grammar for you at your school, Jack,' retorted Mildred.

This biting sarcasm 'shut up' Master Jack for a moment or two, for he was a boy of rather slow ideas. There is no saying, however, what weapons he might not have had recourse to, if just then the carriage had not drawn up at the Willoughbys' own door, considerably to the relief of Joan and the others.

And the next day saw Miss Frost off to her own home at Hexford.

Honor did not succeed in seeing Sheila again that evening. She was already in bed, Ellen said, and probably asleep. She had a bad headache, nurse said, which no one was surprised to hear, as her fits of temper and crying often brought on suffering of the kind. And she had asked not to be disturbed.

'Was there no message for me—no little note or anything?' asked Mrs. Josselin anxiously.

Ellen shook her head, and her mistress sighed. Mrs. Josselin had never known Sheila *quite* so rude and insulting as she had been; for Mildred's presence made it seem far worse, and she had felt sure that the offence would be followed by a corresponding fit of penitence. But no——

'I never dreamt she could have been so hard and obstinate,' thought her mother. 'I really do feel almost in despair.'

To Honor she said as little as she could, trying rather to cheer her by expressing hopes that when Sheila came quite to herself again she would feel more truly sorry than ever before. But after the little girl had gone to bed, Mrs. Josselin had a long and confidential talk with Miss Burke, which ended in her deciding that if Sheila remained in this wretchedly unsatisfactory temper, some step must be taken to bring her to her senses.

Mr. Josselin was late of returning home that night. He had had to attend a political meeting some miles off, and he was rather surprised when he got home to find Mrs. Josselin still up.

'You should not have waited for me,' he said.

'You must be tired after all the exertions for the birthday party. It went off well, I hope?'

'O Arthur,' said Mrs. Josselin, 'it was because all that happened at it that I felt I must sit up to talk to you. I could not have gone to sleep. I am really so thoroughly miserable about Sheila, and about our poor little Honor too. All this is ruining her life; and we have no right to make her so unhappy. I do not think we *can* keep Sheila at home. She must be sent to school.'

Mr. Josselin's face grew very grave.

'Are the servants in bed?' he said. 'No, of course not. Josiah let me in.'

Josiah was a young footman.

'I will just ring and say no one need sit up, if you don't mind,' he went on, 'and then we can talk. I daresay it will rest you more to talk than to try to sleep, with all this worry on your mind.'

'Yes, indeed,' said Mrs. Josselin. 'You understand so well, Arthur; and,' she continued with a little hesitation, after Josiah had received his orders, 'when we have to talk—privately—about the children, I think I feel more at ease if it is late at night. I am always—I really cannot help it, Arthur—I am so nervously afraid of anything being overheard. You don't think it *possible*, do you, that any sort of rumour has come round to Sheila, and that that is the reason of her increased bad temper and jealousy?'

"Impossible!' said Mr. Josselin, 'quite impossible. You are fanciful, Evelyn dear.'

'Perhaps I am. It does seem to grow more and more of a burden—I don't mean the care of the dear child, but the secret. O Arthur, how I wish we had never agreed to it!'

She sighed, and her sigh was re-echoed by her husband.

'So do I—often and often,' he said. 'And yet when I go over it all again it seems as if we had no choice. It was all so hurried. But I want you to tell me about the fresh troubles to-day with Sheila. I see there have been some.'

He had risen and strolled to the window, which was still open. It was a beautiful night, perfectly still and almost too warm. The moon was shining brightly.

'Come outside, Evelyn. It is lovely, and the air will refresh you. We can walk up and down the terrace a little, or sit on the garden chairs if you are tired.'

Mrs. Josselin did as her husband proposed. For

some minutes they paced slowly backwards and forwards, while she related to him Sheila's extraordinary behaviour. Mr. Josselin listened attentively, only interrupting now and then by some question. Then, when he had heard all, he made Mrs. Josselin sit down on the rustic bench just in front of the library window.

'You will certainly be very tired to-morrow,' he said. 'Still, I suppose we must talk it over. Yes, I fear there is nothing for it but to send her away— for a time at least.'

'I fear so,' Mrs. Josselin replied. 'You see what I feel so strongly is that it is not fair to Honor to make *her* life so miserable, as I can see it often is, though the poor child does her best to hide it. She could not be more unselfish than she is.'

'She is very sweet,' Mr. Josselin agreed, 'and that increases our responsibility; and as it is really impossible to lay any blame to Honor's share, I suppose Sheila grows more and more jealous, and accuses us of partiality.'

'And I have *so* striven to be impartial,' said his wife.

'I know you have, and you have been perfectly so. And Miss Burke too. I think she is entirely fair and just. She had no prepossessions of any kind when she came. Of course her knowing the secret would not have made any difference in that way. Still, I am glad we were not free to tell it to her. It might have caused some amount of constraint.'

'Oh!' exclaimed Mrs. Josselin, 'if only there were no secret!'

'You must not exaggerate its effects,' said her husband. 'I do not know that things would have been much better with Sheila even if she had been brought up to know the truth. It is her nature, her own unhappy character, that is the real trouble. And for every one's sake we must try to give her a lesson. Otherwise what still greater trouble may there not be in the future when the secret has to be told? Yes—she has gone too far. We must send her to school. I am convinced of it. It will be a relief to all concerned, and may be—we must of course choose most carefully where to send her—I trust it will be, the saving of the unhappy child.'

Mrs. Josselin did not speak for a moment or two. She was crying quietly to herself.

'I do feel so *terribly* disappointed,' she said. 'If it were not for Honor, I should try still to battle on. But I quite see we must not be unfair to her. I wonder if parents have often trouble like this—I mean with their *own* children. Sometimes it seems to me as if we must have done wrong somehow in accepting the charge of another—and yet——'

'My dearest Evelyn, do try to leave the past,' said Mr. Josselin earnestly. 'We acted for the best and from no selfish motives. What we are now concerned with is the present.'

'Yes,' she said gently, 'I see that. And of course much harm might have come to the poor child if she had been left to the care of her mother's relations. We have saved her from that.'

'We have done our best. The future will show things more clearly. I sometimes doubt if those people—the mother's relations, I mean—*were* as objectionable as the old man believed; but she will be able to judge for herself when she is older.'

'What do you think should be done about Sheila in the meantime? To-morrow, for instance—how is she to be treated?' Mrs. Josselin inquired.

'That depends on herself. If she makes a full and sincere apology in the morning, of course we shall accept it, and let things be as usual, to some extent, till we have found a thoroughly suitable school. If not,' and Mr. Josselin's usually kind voice grew stern and almost hard, 'Sheila must take the consequences. I will not allow you to be insulted and defied with impunity. If no message is sent you in the morning, I think Sheila must be told she must spend the day in her own room.'

'Oh, but I feel *sure* she will be sorry, truly sorry,' said Mrs. Josselin, as she rose from her seat; and as she made her way indoors a hope passed through her mind, that perhaps after all, things had come to the worst and would now begin to improve. 'Sheila is *sure* to be very sorry to-morrow morning,' she said to herself, and with this in her mind she fell asleep.

Her slumbers would have been less peaceful and her dreams more disturbed had she known that almost all, certainly a great part, of her conversation with Mr. Josselin had been overheard by Sheila herself. It had never struck either the father or mother that one of the windows of the girl's room opened above the library, looking down upon the terrace where they had been walking and talking, and the night being so warm, Sheila had kept her window open.

She had no intention of listening to the voices which soon began to reach her ears from the library below. She could not for some time distinguish anything of what was said—not till her father and mother came out on to the terrace did she even know who the speakers were. And just at first when some fragments of their talk began to reach her, she started up, on the point either of calling out that she was awake, and could hear what was said, or of closing the window tight and getting back into bed, where she would have been safe from all temptation to eavesdropping.

But it was not Sheila's good angel who was the nearest to her just then. She was in a bitter and rebellious frame of mind still; full of jealous anger and wounded feelings. Her imagination, too, had been excited by the gypsy's mysterious allusions and Mildred's foolish gossip, and she had really ended by almost persuading herself that she had actual grounds for belief in some strange secret which would explain the unhappiness of her life, for she would not trace it to its true cause.

'They do not love me—none of them really love me,' she had said to herself. 'That is at the root of it all, and if I am soured and embittered, what wonder? If papa and mamma loved me and treated me as they do Honor, I could be sweet and charming too.

No wonder she is so bright and affectionate and everything nice. She gets nothing but praise, and no one crosses her in anything.'

Such had been the thoughts filling the unhappy child's mind as she spent the solitary evening in her room. She fell asleep at last, half-sitting, half-lying on the edge of the bed, dressed as she was, to wake with a start to find herself all in the dark, for the moon had not yet risen. Then she lighted a candle and undressed, getting into bed without saying her prayers, without any of the tender 'good-nights' which are such a sweet and sacred part of daily life. No wonder that her sleep was broken and uneasy, ending after an hour or two in a sudden start into complete wakefulness, so complete that she felt as if she could *never* go to sleep again. And to cool her throbbing head she crept out of bed again and sat down by the open window, staring out at the moonlight and wishing in her petulant, nervous unhappiness that it would go in and let everything be dark outside as in her own discontented little heart.

Then it was that the murmur of voices below first reached her, and when the speakers came out on to the terrace and her own name caught her ear, her first impulse, as I said, was to call out, or to draw back out of hearing—for by nature and instinct there was nothing mean or deceitful about Sheila.

But—the temptation to hear more was irresistible. It almost appeared to her that the opportunity had been put in the way on purpose; and prepossessed as her imagination was already, it was no wonder that every sentence she overheard—though some of the conversation escaped her—seemed to her clearly to point in the one direction, and every moment her agony of curiosity and suspicion increased.

After a few minutes she felt no longer any hesitation.

'They have deceived me all these years,' she thought to herself—'all my life. I am quite justified in listening.'

And listen she did, straining every nerve not to lose a syllable, smiling with a bitterness sad to see on a young face, when she heard the question of sending her to school decided upon; setting her teeth at Mr. Josselin's stern reply to his wife's inquiry about 'to-morrow morning.'

'No, indeed,' she said to herself; 'to-morrow shall see no apology from me—*me* whom they have made so miserable. And no school shall have me as a

And listen she did, straining every nerve not to lose a syllable.—P. 80.

pupil. I can take the law in my own hands now, and I will.'

Only once did any touch of softer feeling come over her in that first hot burst of indignation. It was when Mrs. Josselin's voice repeated more cheerfully, 'I feel *sure* she will be sorry.'

'O mamma, mamma, stop!' cried Sheila in her heart, starting up in a sort of terror lest she had spoken aloud.

Then a strange agony swept over her.

'She is *not* mamma,' she remembered, and, sinking back on her chair, the child lay for some moments in a state of half-unconsciousness.

CHAPTER VI

SHEILA MAKES UP HER MIND

THAT was a terrible night—a night which Sheila never forgot, never will forget, even if she live to be a very old woman.

She must have crept back to bed somehow, after a while, without knowing it; for the next thing she was conscious of was the awaking suddenly from a deep, stupefying sleep—a sleep so deep that for some moments she felt in a kind of chaos; she could not tell where she was nor even who she was.

Then gradually things cleared a little, and she woke to the knowledge that something was wrong, *quite* wrong, terribly wrong.

What was it?

She had had the feeling before — often, to a certain extent, on awaking, the morning after one of her fits of temper, when conscience had insisted on making itself heard; once or twice when real trouble had come near her. There was that time when papa and mamma were coming from London, and there was an accident to the train which delayed it, and the little girls had gone to bed in much anxiety. How they had clung together that night, and how lovely it was when the fears, returning again with the morning light, were quickly dispersed by the sight of dear mamma herself at the door—a little pale and tired, but 'all right,' and *so* eager to comfort her little girls; and that other time when Honor had scarlet fever and Sheila was not allowed to see her for so long, and there came a day when the doctor scarcely left the house and mamma's eyes were red with crying, and Sheila scarcely dared to whisper 'how is she?' when she awoke the next morning.

Why did these memories come to torment her as she gradually recalled the present misery; why could she not feel *only* hard and bitter and almost wildly indignant?

'O mamma, mamma,' burst out the poor child, even while she tried to choke the words down, 'I *have* loved you, I have loved you terribly, and papa too, and dear little Honor. And to think you are not mine—that you have never been mine—that I belong to nobody! Oh, why have you deceived me so, and pretended to care for me, when you didn't? Oh, it is too awful, too dreadful!'

And the hard anger came back again. It was not the shock of the discovery that caused it, so much as the long train of miserable jealousies and tempers of which the sad truth she had overheard, now seemed to her to have all along been the cause and the excuse. If she had been on happier terms with them all, *trust* would have stepped in at this crisis. She would have told what she had heard, and believed that for all which seemed so strange and startling there was some explanation, some good reason.

But as things were, this was the very last course which Sheila was likely to take. She was still, in much, very childish. She did not begin wondering who, if not Mr. and Mrs. Josselin's child, she really was, or what had been the motive for the secret. She did not say to herself that her parents, or those she had thought her parents, had probably adopted her out of goodness, and that if she knew all she would only find more, not less cause for love and gratitude. She was determined to see everything the wrong way. She had been deceived all her life; she had been disliked and despised, and expected to give love and respect to those who did not care for her, and only thought her a burden, and she was not to blame for her faults. Just at present she did not feel as if she cared who she was, or where she had come from, or what became of her. Her whole mind was filled with one idea—to get away—away from her home and her friends for ever. She would make her own way somehow; they should never be troubled with her again, and *then* perhaps—then when it was too late—they would be sorry.

Where should she go? She was sensible enough to know that she could not run away to nowhere. Unless she made some kind of plan she would certainly be found and brought back again in disgrace, and things would be worse than ever. She would be sent to school, and as this thought struck her, Sheila started up in bed as if she would like to run away that moment. Sent to school, like a naughty girl, to be reformed!

'No, indeed,' she thought, '*that* I will never submit to. Very likely the schoolmistress would be told I was only an object of charity, a poor child picked up somewhere or other, and who was turning out quite unworthy of all that had been done for her. Why did they pick me up? Why didn't they leave me wherever I was? It would have been far kinder in the end than to take me and not love me.'

Not love her? Sheila's conscience was not dead. The words startled her. Was it true that they had not loved her? All sorts of memories came pressing up — acts of tenderness, words and tones which nothing but 'love' could explain—little plans for giving her pleasure, gentle touches and caresses too often ungraciously received, if not rudely repulsed. Had she *not* been loved? The very earnestness with which her faults had been pointed out to her, the almost solemn warnings as to what her jealous, unbridled temper might become if she did not learn to curb it—were not all these things proofs of love, of real devotion?

But Sheila would not listen.

'They thought it their duty to try to bring me up well, I suppose. I don't mean to say that papa and mamma——' and again that agony of remembering that she had no right to use those names—'Mr. and Mrs. Josselin, I should say,' she corrected bitterly, 'are not good people. I suppose they adopted me out of goodness. But I would have been happier in the poorest cottage with those who truly cared for me.'

And so her thoughts went round and round the same miserable circle during the weary hours till morning came, for it was only between three and four when she awoke, and the stable clock striking seven found her still tossing about feverishly, unable to forget her miseries.

After all, however, she did fall asleep again for a little. Honor peeped in on her way downstairs at eight and saw that Sheila was slumbering, though by the way she turned about and murmured and moaned it was evident that her sleep was not very refreshing.

But Honor did not wake her, and in answer to Mrs. Josselin's inquiries the little girl said that she was sure Sheila would awake with one of her headaches.

Miss Burke was her next visitor. She had come by Mrs. Josselin's desire, she told Sheila, to know if anything was the matter; if she was ill, her breakfast should be sent up to her.

'No, thank you,' said Sheila calmly. 'I am not ill. I have only got a little headache. I don't want any breakfast.'

'That is nonsense, my dear,' said the young

governess. 'If you are not ill you must have something to eat. Is your head aching?'

'A little. I have not slept well,' Sheila replied.

'Then I will send you up some tea and toast anyway,' said Miss Burke, as she turned to leave the room.

She hesitated for a moment as she got to the door.

'Sheila, dear,' she said very gently, 'have you not—cannot I take any message from you to your mamma?'

A strange impulse seized Sheila. She was feeling so very, very miserable. Supposing she made a confidante of her governess and asked for her advice. But the idea was dismissed almost as soon as it entered her mind.

No; she wanted no friend, and no advice *here*. Miss Burke would very probably not believe her, and would think it some mad fancy born of the jealousy and ill-temper she was always being accused of. Besides, as a better motive for silence occurred to her, had she any right to tell the secret here in their own house to any one but Mr. or Mrs. Josselin themselves? And that, oh, that she *could* not do!

So she only turned her head on the pillow, with

what looked to Miss Burke like sulky obstinacy, as she replied—

'No, I have not any message to send. None at all.'

The young governess sighed as she hurried downstairs.

'Her temper is really terrible,' she thought. 'I am afraid she will have to be sent away.'

All that morning Sheila spent in her room alone. After her breakfast she got up and dressed, nurse coming to help her as usual; but she did not speak to Sheila more than was necessary, and Sheila said nothing to her, till just as Ellen was leaving the room, she said—

'I was to say to you, Miss Sheila, that if you wish to speak to your mamma, you can go downstairs to the library, where you will find her alone.'

'I do not wish to speak to her,' Sheila replied.

'Then I am afraid you will have to stay here all day, till your papa comes home in the evening. Those were his orders, unless your mamma gave others after seeing you.'

'Thank you. It is exactly what I expected. I am quite prepared to stay here all day,' said Sheila coolly.

And old Ellen sighed too, like Miss Burke, as she left the room. Her sighs were even deeper, for she was very grieved for her master and mistress.

She was the only person in the house who had their full confidence and understood all the difficulties of their position, and how patiently and wisely they had met them.

One other effort was made to soften the unhappy child, and in permitting it Mrs. Josselin felt that she was doing almost more than was perhaps right. It was through Honor.

Poor Honor was very unhappy. She had never been quite so unhappy before. *Somehow*, it seemed to her, this very bad fit of naughtiness of Sheila's was of her causing. It had to do with her birthday —could she, Honor, not have done something to prevent it? Had she not been loving and grateful enough? Had she thought too much of her own enjoyment and put her sister aside in some hurting way?

She went over and over these ideas in her mind, even though she could not succeed in blaming herself, as she was always ready to do, and then she begged to be allowed to go to see Sheila, so wistfully and tearfully that Mrs. Josselin could not refuse her.

'Perhaps I've vexed her without meaning it,' she said. 'O mamma dear, *do* let me run up to her just for one moment. Papa *wouldn't* mind.'

Sheila was standing by the window, looking out, and apparently doing nothing, when Honor's timid knock sounded at the door. Sheila had locked it.

'At least I will have my room to myself,' she had thought, 'if I am to spend all day in it.'

And before she drew back the bolt, she hurriedly threw her writing-case, on which lay a half-written letter, on to the bed, drawing the little eider-down coverlet over them; then, stepping back quietly, she called out—

'Come in, I have unfastened the door.'

A fair-haired head, with an anxious little face, peeped in timidly.

'Sheila,' whispered Honor, 'Sheila dear, may I come in?'

'I *told* you to come in,' said the elder girl coldly, without looking towards her. 'What do you want?'

Honor came forward quietly, without speaking, but when, not hearing her approach, Sheila turned round, and the little girl caught sight of her pale face and blue-encircled eyes, all telling of a disturbed or sleepless night and suffering none the less real that it was self-caused, even her fear of Sheila vanished before her sympathy.

'O darling,' she exclaimed, rushing forward and flinging her arms round her sister's neck, 'you *do* look so ill and unhappy! Dear, dear Sheila—why won't you be sweet and loving? Have I vexed you —is it my fault?' and the tears rained down her face.

Sheila did not repulse her, but neither did she respond. She gently loosened Honor's arms, and, drawing forward another chair, made her sit down beside her.

'Please don't cry so, Honor,' she said. 'It—it will only make things worse for me. No—it is not your fault. You cannot help it all, you cannot love me. I am not lovable. I—I understand it now. I have a bad nature. I am proud and, I suppose, selfish. I think I might have been different if I had had a better chance; at least—no, I can't explain, and it is no use, *now*.'

'What do you mean, Sheila?' said Honor, amidst her sobs. 'Why do you say "*now*"? There's nothing new. Why shouldn't we begin again fresh, and try to be happy and not vex each other? Oh, do say you will, Sheila, darling Sheila, and then we can remember my birthday happily after all?'

Sheila was touched, deeply touched. Never had she been so near to believing that she was really and truly loved. But for that terrible discovery, but for the conversation she had overheard in what seemed now like a dreadful nightmare, she would, I think, have given in—have crushed down her hard pride and resolved to try again. She turned her head away so that Honor should not see the tears that *would* come; then she recalled some of Mr. Josselin's words, and summoned her bitter resentment to her aid.

'I am to be sent to school to be reformed,' she thought. 'They wish they were free from the burden of me. How can I feel love or gratitude? No, no, there is only one thing to do.'

But she could not be hard or resentful to the little weeping creature beside her. Sheila's nature had a great reserve of large protecting love for the suffering and pitiable, as I have said, and just now Honor's tear-stained face and trembling frame appealed to this best side of her.

'My poor little Onnie,' she said, using the pet name of their baby days, while in her turn she threw her arms round her sister,—'my poor little Onnie, I do believe you love me, and indeed, indeed, I love you.'

'Then you *will* speak to mamma and tell her— tell her you want to try again?' said Honor eagerly.

But instantly Sheila stiffened.

'No,' she said, 'I cannot, and I will not.'

So after all it was with fresh tears and sad disappointment that Honor left her, to report to Mrs. Josselin how she too had failed.

'But she was very loving to me, mamma,' she said, 'very loving.'

And the remembrance of Sheila's rare caress grew very precious to the little girl in the days that were to come.

But to Mrs. Josselin it only added to her perplexity about Sheila to be told of her showing this affection to Honor while remaining so obdurate and unfeeling towards her parents.

After Honor had left her, Sheila felt instinctively that she had refused her last chance; she had, so to say, burnt her boats.

'They will not try anything like that again,' she thought. 'Most likely I shall be sent off to school almost at once. So I had better make haste.'

She bolted her door again, though feeling pretty sure that she would be left undisturbed till dinner-time. Then she drew out her writing-case and added a word or two to the almost completed letter, which she folded and placed in an envelope addressed to—

'Miss Mildred Frost,
    Hexford,
      ——shire.'

And having done this, she sat down again and proceeded to consider her plans.

She had between two and three pounds in her purse, for since her last birthday she had begun to have a little allowance for small needs, such as gloves and hair ribbons, and the birthday presents whose value is doubled when you feel they have been bought 'with my own money.'

This was enough, and more than enough, to take her to Mildred's home, and once there she trusted to her friend to help her in some way or other.

'I am too young to be a governess, even a nursery governess,' she said to herself, 'but I should think I might easily go to some school where I could help to teach the little ones and have some lessons myself'—an arrangement she had read of in some of her story-books. 'Of course I will change my name. After all,' with another of those dreadful twinges, 'it *isn't* my name, so I need not mind. I will call myself something quite common—Barber or Roberts. No, Robins; yes, Robins will do, and it isn't really ugly when you think of the redbreasts. Robins. But I cannot go till to-morrow. Mildred was not *quite* certain herself of going to-day, though the gypsy said so. I may not be able to go till the day after. Perhaps that would be best. I'll alter my letter,' and taking it out again, she did so. '"Expect me by the first train I could get to Hexford by from here on *Friday*," she wrote—" the first train that gets through by leaving Mandy Station after nine, for I don't think I could get there earlier, as it is quite two miles off." That will be best. And now I must get this letter posted. How can I get to the post?'

She considered. After all, there was no great practical difficulty. She had been told to stay in her room; she had not promised that she would.

'Mamma—Mrs. Josselin, I mean—is sure to go out this afternoon. Very likely she will take Honor and Miss Burke with her, as she did that other day that I was sent up here—the day I tore our duet in two, ever so long ago—to cheer Honor up. I'll wait till I hear the carriage drive out and then I'll see. I'll keep my door bolted and go out by the one on the back passage, and lock it outside; there is a key. So that if nurse or any one comes they'll just think I'm in a worse temper than ever, and that I won't let them in. And then—can't I do anything else? Yes, I know what. I'll make a bundle of the clothes I must take, and I'll hide it in one of the hollow trees in the little wood, so that it will be there all ready on Friday morning. The wood is the best way to go through to the lane, for the people about are all rather frightened of it,' and Sheila laughed scornfully.

This plan she proceeded to prepare for, taking, strange to say, a curious pleasure in choosing the things she thought the most suitable, feeling herself by fits and starts quite a heroine—glad, I suppose, to find anything to do to stifle the cruel stabbing pain in her heart, which still every now and then made itself felt.

And between three and four in the afternoon, having heard the carriage drive out, and the whole house sounding perfectly silent, Sheila carried out her plan. She bolted one door inside, and locked the second one—through which she made her way downstairs—on the outside, taking the key with her, and then, her bundle under her arm and the letter to Mildred in her pocket, she stole out, choosing the least frequented paths in the shrubbery till she reached the little wood.

CHAPTER VII

IN THE GYPSY CARAVAN

SHEILA hurried on as fast as she could till she got to a part of the wood where she knew there were two or three old trees, one of which had been struck by lightning many, many years before, and had a great hollow inside, which the children used to call to themselves 'the witch's cupboard.'

Here she had decided to leave her bundle. She had tied her things up neatly in a large dark-coloured silk handkerchief, for she could not have got a bag or small box of any kind, except by asking nurse for it; and besides this, she reflected that the lighter her luggage was to carry, the better.

She found the tree without difficulty and hid the package in it, looking round her, after doing so, to make sure that there was no one about who could possibly have seen her movements. The afternoon was very still; there was not a sound except the occasional faint note of a bird, or the tiny rustle of a falling leaf.

'It is all right,' thought Sheila, and she was just turning away to go into the post-office, when a slight, very slight, but distinct *scrunching* sound on the dry, crisp soil made her stop. Some one was coming towards her.

Sheila was not frightened, for she was naturally not the least cowardly. But she was afraid of being seen or interfered with. Suddenly the sound stopped, and again all was perfectly still. Sheila waited some moments, however, to make sure. Then, becoming satisfied that the steps she had heard must have been those of some one crossing the wood in another direction, she set off again, walking fast, though cautiously; for she had more than a mile to go, after leaving the wood, before she could reach the village where she meant to post her letter.

But, fast as she walked there was some one behind, who managed not to lose sight of her—some one who, once the girl had emerged on to the road, scarcely more than a lane, along which lay Sheila's way, crept stealthily by the other side of the hedge, keeping up with her, though unseen, till they were within a

Crept stealthily by the other side of the hedge, keeping up with her, though unseen.—P. 100.

short distance of the village. Then the somebody, a small bent old figure in a red cloak, wonderfully alert and nimble, though to judge by her looks she might have been a hundred years old, suddenly hastened her steps, hurrying over a field just where the road turned a little, and scrambling through or over the gate on to the footpath. Then she stood for a moment to recover her breath, while still out of Sheila's view, and then walked back slowly to meet her, to all appearances as if she were coming from the village.

Sheila, who had been pacing along with her eyes on the ground for some minutes, her thoughts absorbed, started a little, when something—she could not have said what—made her look up and she caught sight of the figure calmly advancing towards her. She gave no sign of her surprise nevertheless, and walked on, quickening her pace, meaning to pass the gypsy without any notice except a nod.

But she had reckoned without her host. Old Diana was not to be set aside. She planted herself on the path right in front of Sheila, with a calm smile on her face.

'So my pretty one is off to the post-office all by herself,' she said coolly, and this time Sheila could not conceal her start. She grew red with vexation too, and was on the point of replying angrily, when Diana stopped her by speaking again, this time in a different tone.

'I know all about it, my young lady,' she said gravely. 'I knew it would come, and it has come. But you are a child. Do you think the village people will not notice you and your letter? You have to buy a stamp'—this was a lucky shot of the sharp old woman's—'and they will be sure to talk about the young lady from the Hall coming in for one stamp. I'll tell you what to do. Let me post the letter for you. I'll be as quick as you could be and quicker. You needn't give it me till we're past the turn of the road, in sight of the shop; and you can see me put it in the box if you stand by the hedge, where no one will see you.'

Sheila was too surprised at first to speak. Then the sense of what Diana had said struck her. The people at the post-office certainly would know her.

'What do you want to know all about me for?' she said. 'Why should you offer to help me?'

'There's reasons for most things,' said the gypsy. 'You're in trouble, and some day maybe you'll come out of it, and then you can do old Diana a good turn.

I don't think much of the quarter you're seeking help from now, but young folk must live and learn.'

She walked on again, retracing her steps as she spoke, and Sheila half mechanically stepped along beside her. And in a few moments, when they were within a short distance of the shop, standing at the extreme end of the village, which was also the post-office, she found herself handing her letter and the penny for a stamp to the gypsy, though how she came to give in to her advice so easily she afterwards could hardly explain.

In two minutes the old woman was beside her again, the errand accomplished.

'Thank you, thank you very much,' said Sheila, but she did not offer money to the gypsy. Somehow she felt as if it might offend her.

Diana smiled.

'You're going home again,' she said. 'I will take you part of the way.'

'No, thank you,' said Sheila. 'It's not the way to the common, and I can go quite well alone. Good-bye.'

The gypsy was not offended. She only smiled.

'Your way's mine for the present,' she said; 'and is it to-morrow you are going off to your friend?'

'No,' said Sheila thoughtlessly, 'not till the day after. Mildred will only get my letter to-morrow, and, indeed, I'm not sure that she's gone home.'

Then she stopped suddenly, wondering at herself for having told so much. Diana read her thoughts.

'You've told me naught but what I know,' she said coolly, nodding her head. 'Oh yes, she's gone. I told her she'd go to-day. And you know more than when I saw you yesterday—yes, much more, though there is still much to know.'

Sheila stood still and turned almost fiercely upon the old woman.

'Will you speak out once for all and tell me what you mean?' she said.

To her surprise Diana answered very gravely—

'I cannot. But you are very foolish. If you want to carry out your plan you had better stay out now you are out. Tell me what you mean to do.'

She spoke with a tone almost of command, and Sheila obeyed her. She told the old woman all that had happened—her own misery of the night before, the solitary day she had spent, and her determination to run away.

The old woman listened attentively. By this time they were close to the wood. She took Sheila gently by the arm and drew her well within the shade of the trees, and then she talked to her quickly and eagerly, in a low voice, though there was no one near to hear, the girl scarcely interrupting by word or sign till she left off.

Then Sheila stood gravely considering for a moment or two; she had grown even paler, though she was pale enough before. Old Diana's words had brought home to her with a new pang of misery the truth of the discovery she believed herself to have made, though the gypsy refused to say anything more as to the grounds for her mysterious hints.

'You must decide, my young lady,' said Diana at last. 'If you mean to do this you can only do it with my help. If you try to manage it for yourself you will be caught and brought back in disgrace long before you've got to Hexford.'

The girl sighed deeply.

'I daresay I should be,' she said. 'Well, then, I will come with you. I don't know why you want to help me. I suppose you are doing it out of kindness, and I suppose I should thank you; but I am so miserable I can't think of anything except getting away.'

'We must be quick, then,' said Diana. 'I know

where your bundle is—you meant to leave it there till the day after to-morrow; and supposing it had poured with rain, as I daresay it will before night, your clothes wouldn't have been much use to you once they were well soaked.'

'I pushed them a good way into the tree. I think they would have kept dry,' said Sheila, in a dull, indifferent voice.

Diana took no notice of her manner. She hurried on to the hollow tree, Sheila following her more slowly, and in a few moments the old woman came towards her again, the packet in her arms.

'Now,' she said, 'we must be off, and we must put our best foot foremost too, if we're to make up to the others before dark. They'll have got half an hour's start at the least.'

She led the way out of the wood, crossing the road almost at once, and plunging into the smaller lanes, of which there were a great many in that part of the country. Sheila knew her way well, of course, as Curlew Moor had been her home as long as she could remember; but after they had walked a mile or two she began to feel a little puzzled. Diana went on steadily, not showing the least sign of fatigue, and seeming as sure of her way as if she were a native born and bred. She scarcely spoke, and Sheila, plunged in her own gloomy thoughts, was not sorry to be left to herself, till she began to feel very tired. She was not used to show patience or endurance, and she turned to her guide complainingly.

'Have we much farther to go?' she said. 'You said it would not be far, and that then I should drive in one of the vans.'

Diana glanced at her. She saw that the girl was looking very fagged, and she thought to herself that Sheila was not of the make of those who can battle their way in the world.

'We've not come four miles yet,' she said. 'At your age, missie, I could have got over four times four without turning a hair. And even now I can manage half that and none the worse for it, at a stretch. But we're close to the road now. Across those fields and we'll be at it, and then we can rest a bit till the vans come up.'

They had not very long to wait; but Sheila was so tired that, in spite of everything, she would probably have fallen asleep, sitting there on the grass at the edge of the road, beside the old woman, had it been much longer. Soon, however, they heard the sound of slow-coming wheels, the groaning and rumbling of heavy conveyances, and then the gypsy caravan hove in sight.

There were three vans, a few men and boys walking alongside each, and in the two last several women and children of different ages. But they moved on very silently; there was no talk or laughter to be heard; even the dogs tied beneath the vans seemed sober and depressed. Old Diana had but to show herself on the road for the whole cavalcade to come to a halt.

She opened the door at the back of the first waggon, and signed to Sheila to mount up. This waggon, to Sheila's satisfaction, was without any passengers. It was hung, within and without, all round, with baskets and brushes and wicker-work chairs and the like, and it seemed fairly clean. There was a little space at the farthest-in end, where stood a small table and an old wooden chair with a red cushion.

'Sit ye down,' said Diana. 'This is where I stay when I want to be alone, and none of the children may disturb me here. They'll not disturb you either, and the less you show yourself outside the better.'

Sheila sank wearily on to the seat.

'And you'll take me to the railway station on the

way to Hexford the morning after to-morrow. You *promise* me?' she said to the old woman.

'Yes, I've promised you faithful, and I'll keep my word. And now I'll get you a cup of tea and a bite of something to eat. And I'll settle a bed for you in here all cosy, my pretty.'

She was much more caressing in her way to Sheila now. She seemed brimful of delight and a kind of triumph. If Sheila had been less stupefied by fatigue and a sort of reaction from the excitement she had been going through, she would probably have been more struck than she was by the change in the gypsy's manner, and would have wondered what was the reason of it.

Diana had a strange effect on her. Sheila had never felt afraid of her like Mildred, but she had very soon given in to the old woman, with a docility she had scarcely ever shown to any one in her life. No doubt Diana had a very strong character and a personal influence it is difficult to explain — an influence possessed by many of her race, and often probably used for bad and selfish purposes. When she fixed her bright, keen dark eyes on Sheila, the girl felt as if she had no wish to stand out against anything the gypsy proposed, and now that she was utterly exhausted and tired, this feeling was still stronger. And Diana, with the experience of her great age, knew well that the girl was in her power, and was glad of it.

But to prevent any misunderstanding, I think it is, perhaps, best here to explain that the old gypsy was not a bad or selfish woman. She had had a strange life, she came of a race so unlike ours that we can scarcely understand their ideas about right and wrong, she had been taught nothing except what she had taught herself. Nevertheless, in many ways, she might have served as an example to those who have had a thousand times her advantages. She was brave and courageous past words, she had a heart which could love tenderly; above all, she was capable of the most intense and undying gratitude. And in all her conduct to Sheila this—this extraordinary passion of gratitude—was, as you will see, her motive.

She was growing fond of the girl for her own sake too. And just now the sight of the poor child with her white face and wistful eyes went to the gypsy's heart.

'The pretty dear,' she said to herself as she went off to one of the other vans, 'no wonder she looks pined and weary, and no wonder her temper's crossed with the way those cold, proud folk have put upon her. But she shall hold her own yet and be with her own, if old Diana's alive to see to it.'

Then a different expression came over her face.

'I wish she had favoured her own folk more,' she thought. 'She's not like either father or mother, for he was a ruddy man, and her mother was pink and white, with blue eyes and golden hair like a fairy; and she's not got her mother's sweet laughing ways neither. But that will come maybe.'

A few minutes later Sheila, already almost half asleep, was aroused by the return of the old woman, followed by a handsome dark-complexioned girl of thirteen or fourteen, one of Diana's great-granddaughters, carrying a jug and cup and some other little things. Diana herself drew out a mattress and covered it with a large soft rug and made Sheila lie down upon it, which the tired girl was nothing loth to do. Then she carefully—tenderly indeed—took off Sheila's boots, and covered her over with another rug or shawl, and, turning to the young gypsy, took from her the jug and poured out a cupful of hot steaming liquid which she called 'tea.'

'Drink this, my pretty,' she said. 'It will take

the aches out of your bones and you will wake as
fresh as a lark, and with her usual strange obedience
to the old woman's wishes, Sheila sat half up and
drank it.

It had a pleasant fragrant taste and odour, but
'tea' in our common sense of the word it certainly
was not. It was probably decocted from some herbs
known to the gypsies—for they are wise in such
lore. Be that as it may it seemed to soothe Sheila
almost magically. She drank it all, and then lay
down again, her head resting on a cushion which
Diana had drawn out from some of her mysterious
receptacles.

'Thank you,' she said sleepily, 'that is funny tea,
but it is very nice.'

And then she knew no more, her sleep being even
untroubled by dreams; and never since her baby-
hood had the girl been more devotedly watched than
by the old gypsy, till long after the daylight had
faded, first into the red-streaked grey of an autumn
evening, and then into the darkness of a cloudy
night; while the vans jogged and creaked along the
road, and all but Diana herself and the men con-
ducting them were asleep.

It was not often they travelled on like this. But

the old woman who was really the ruling spirit of the society had her reasons for it. An hour or two after midnight she rose from her place by Sheila and looked out to give her orders.

'We shall be at Fool's Corner long before dawn,' she said. 'We shall camp there, as I told you, for the day. Then you can take your turn of a rest, boys, and make the others bestir themselves.'

'All right, mother,' came the reply.

'I'm going to sleep now,' she went on. 'If you hear anything that seems as if we were being followed, wake me at once.'

'All right,' was the answer again.

'I don't think there's any fear now,' thought Diana.

CHAPTER VIII

A POOR FRIEND IN NEED

IT was broad daylight when Sheila awoke. She felt perfectly well and rested; she had no headache or sensation of discomfort of any kind. But when she first opened her eyes she thought she was dreaming —for some moments she could not conceive where she was. She was lying in a little space cleared out among the baskets, but still they were hanging all around her, and a little streak of morning sun caught the bright colours with which some of the wicker-work things were striped, making them look to her but half-awakened eyes grotesque and fantastic. By degrees it all came back to her, and with a sort of groan she flung herself down again, for she had half sat up, and shut her eyes as if that would shut out the knowledge of her misery. She was alone in the van, and as she began again to take notice of the things about her, she realised that she was no longer moving—everything was perfectly still.

'They must have camped somewhere,' she thought. 'I wonder where Diana is—surely she cannot be playing me any trick? I should die of terror if I were left alone among the other gypsies. And to-day I am to get the train to Hexford and go to Mildred.' With the thought of Mildred came a little comfort, but it quickly faded again. 'No, it's not till to-morrow. What *shall* I do all day shut into this place? And I've not even undressed, and I can't have a bath. Oh, how horrid it is! But I suppose if I hadn't come away like this they'd have found me again at once and I'd have been sent to school.'

This thought brought back her resolution. *Anything* would be better than to be sent off to school 'to be reformed,' as she called it, and to have to continue to consider as her home the house where she had convinced herself no one loved her or cared for her, where now, indeed, she told herself she had no right to be.

But still—habit is very, very strong. Sheila

loved her home and those in it much more deeply than she knew. What were they all thinking about her? she asked herself. She must have been missed long before this—would they care? Honor would, of that she felt sure. Poor little Onnie!

'Perhaps they've guessed that I have found out about the secret,' she said to herself. 'I remember ma—no, Mrs. Josselin, I mean—said that night'— only the night before last, and it seemed to Sheila long years ago!—'that she wondered if any rumour of the truth had come round to me and caused my increased jealousy and ill-temper.' She thought over the words to herself with great bitterness. 'Well, now perhaps she will see how shameful it was to deceive me so. To think what it has driven me to!'

She got up and looked about her. She was growing conscious now that she was very hungry, for she had really eaten nothing since her early dinner the day before, though the 'tea' Diana had given her had been strengthening as well as calming. But Diana had not forgotten her. Just as Sheila was asking herself if she should open the door and look out, she heard a soft tap upon it from the outside.

'Yes,' she called out, 'I am awake!' and the old woman entered.

She looked at the girl critically with her keen eyes.

'You have slept well,' she said. 'You are rested, and you are hungry? Ah! that is well. Your breakfast is ready.'

And then the door opened again and the same girl came in with a basin of steaming hot bread-and-milk.

'Yes, I am very hungry,' said Sheila. 'But I haven't undressed. I feel so messy, Diana, and I want to wash myself.'

'Eat first,' said the old woman, who, though she really was not dirty, did not understand the necessity of feeling oneself clean and tidy if one was to enjoy a meal; and Sheila, fastidious as she was, had to give in.

She ate with a good appetite, and the food was good and carefully prepared. Diana stood by with pleasure in her face.

'I knew she would like it. *They* used to have it so,' she murmured.

Then when the bowl was empty, she gave it to the girl to take away, adding some directions in a curious language which Sheila had never heard before, though in a few minutes its meaning grew plain, as

Matti—that was what Diana called her—reappeared with a little pewter tub and a jug filled with hot water, and a coarse, though clean towel.

'And here is your bundle,' said Diana, bringing it out of a corner, 'so now you can make yourself as neat as a queen, my pretty. And when you want me, you need only call out of the window; I'll hear.'

It was all like a strange, ridiculous dream. But Sheila was glad to feel fresh and tidy again.

'What would Honor think if she could see me?' she thought. 'What fun it will be to tell her all about it!'

But then came back the thought that most likely she would never see Honor again, and with something between a sob and a groan Sheila tried to stifle the bitter misery that seemed as if it would choke her.

She scarcely saw any of the other gypsies; and it struck her as strange that the encampment was so silent. She had always fancied that gypsies were noisy and merry, but these people were very quiet, almost solemn. Towards afternoon they moved on again, travelling till late in the evening. Part of the way the road lay through very pretty woods, and Sheila got Diana to let her walk now and then for a

Gathered flowers and tinted autumn leaves for Sheila.—P. 119.

change. But no one spoke to her except the old woman and Matti, and the latter said very little, though she smiled pleasantly, and gathered flowers and tinted autumn leaves for Sheila.

When they stopped for the night, Diana told her that they were now within an hour of the railway station she had promised to bring her to, and that they would make their way there directly after breakfast the next morning.

And so it came to pass that, before the sun was high in the sky that Friday, Sheila found herself walking along a country road, Diana beside her, on their way to Middleburn to catch the train for Hexford.

'We have plenty of time,' said the old woman; 'the train is not near yet. And what will you do then, when you get to Hexford?'

'Go straight to my friend, of course,' said Sheila. 'She will advise me what to do. I shall stay with her for a few days, till I make my plans.'

The old woman smiled rather peculiarly, but Sheila did not pay much attention to her. She knew that Diana had taken a dislike to Mildred.

'Ah, well,' said the gypsy again, after a little silence, 'so be it. But I have something to say to you, my pretty, before we part. It is well always to have more than one arrow in your quiver. If your friend fails you, if you are in perplexity and distress——'

'Don't make me promise to come back to you,' Sheila interrupted, 'for if I did I should have to keep to it. And though you have been very kind to me, Diana, very, very kind, I couldn't become a gypsy, or go on living as you do. I want to learn to be independent and make my own way. I don't want any one to be able to mock at me.'

Diana nodded.

'I was not going to say what you think. All I want you to know is this. *If* your friends at Hexford fail you, and you are in doubt and distress, there are those near by who would be good to you and help you, better than any strangers could. Remember this — say it after me — Mr. John Flowers, Moorecroft, near Lexing.'

'Mr. John Flowers, Moorecroft, near Lexing,' repeated Sheila mechanically; 'yes, I won't forget.' But she said it more to please Diana than with any intention of ever acting upon this advice, and it was not till afterwards that she wondered what the old woman had meant by the expression 'better than any *strangers*.'

Diana seemed satisfied, however. And while still at some little distance from the station, she bade the girl farewell, saying it was better for her now to make her way alone. She took Sheila's two hands in hers and kissed them, murmuring some words in the strange tongue she had used to Matti, which Sheila could not, of course, understand, though they sounded like a charm or a blessing. And some indefinable feeling made Sheila stoop down to the strange, wrinkled old face with a sudden impulse, very unusual to her, and press a kiss upon the withered cheek, and as she stood up again, she saw that the wonderfully bright eyes were full of tears.

But in another moment the gypsy was gone, making her way so quickly along the road that she seemed out of sight before Sheila realised that she was alone.

A quarter of an hour later the girl was in a second-class compartment of the train, whizzing away to Hexford.

It was well for her purpose that it was not a crowded day on the line ; had she had several fellow-passengers, her appearance, especially with the bundle she carried, would pretty surely have attracted notice. As it was, however, no one paid much attention to her. She, on her side, was in complete ignorance that a few carriages from hers in the train, a swarthy-complexioned, dark-eyed lad of fifteen or thereabouts was sitting composedly in a third-class compartment, having, like herself, taken a ticket to Hexford at Middleburn Station.

The journey took about two hours, though the train was a fast one. Arrived at Hexford, Sheila, bundle in hand, made her way half timidly out of the station. Now that she was so near the goal she had set before herself she began to have misgivings. Would Mildred and her family receive her cordially? And how was she to find out the house? She now remembered that Mildred had given her no address beyond 'Hexford,' which she said was enough. It might be that the Frosts' house was some way out of the town—which way should she go? The station was at one end of a road leading thither from Hexford, and apparently going no farther. Sheila felt afraid of inquiring where Mr. Frost lived. It would seem so odd to arrive from a distance and not know where to go. She *had* had vague hopes of Mildred's meeting her at the station.

While she stood there hesitating, a boy, a dark-haired and dark-eyed young fellow, stepped up to her.

'Carry your bundle, miss?' he said. 'I'll do it for twopence.'

Evidently he thought the bundle the cause of her perplexity, and she took advantage of it.

'Very well,' she said, 'you may carry it, and I'll give you twopence when we get to Mr. Frost's. Do you know where his house is?'

The boy nodded. Truth to tell, he had informed himself about it from a fellow-passenger, an inhabitant of Hexford. But Sheila thought herself very lucky.

'You can walk on with my bundle in front of me,' she said.

The boy nodded again and obeyed her, smiling to himself. He thought she wanted to keep an eye on her possessions, whereas the idea that her guide could have designs upon them had never, in her inexperience, occurred to her.

He walked on, she following, straight down the short stretch of road, bordered by scattered cottages or villas, till he reached the town. Then he made direct for the market-place, pulling up at the door of a small, old-fashioned, but neat house in one corner of the little square. Two stumpy trees stood in the tiny strip of green before the door—Mildred's 'pollards'—and though Sheila half gasped at finding that Mildred's home was so different to what she had pictured it, there was no room for doubt. For on a brightly polished brass plate on the door stood in unmistakable black letters the name—

'Mr. EVERARD FROST,
Solicitor.'

Sheila knocked. Then, recollecting her guide, she turned and took the packet from him, giving him the coppers she had promised. He smiled and thanked her, his white teeth gleaming in his sunburnt face; but he still stood waiting. There seemed some delay in answering the door, and Sheila, nervous and always easily irritated, vented her annoyance on the boy.

'You needn't wait,' she said; 'I'm not going to give you any more.'

He smiled again, quite as amiably as before, and, touching his cap, moved off. But Sheila did not see that he only changed his quarters to the shadow of a neighbouring house, whence unobserved he could still keep her in view. He did not wait long, however. In another minute the door opened, and after a short colloquy with the neat parlour-maid, the stranger was admitted, and the house relapsed into its usual sleepy quiet.

Thereupon the boy decamped, hurrying back to the station as fast as his very nimble legs could carry him, so as to catch a train in a different direction — namely, for Lexing, to which place he took a third-class ticket, and as he seated himself he felt with his hand in the inner pocket of his coat, where it came in contact with a letter.

'All right,' he said to himself, 'Granny won't have called me a sharp lad for nothing.'

Sheila meanwhile had been ushered into a small, rather prim and unused-looking, but very neat — everything about the house was neat — drawing-room. She was too anxious to take much notice of anything — something in the air made her conscious that this was not the rapturous greeting she had been counting upon. Half mechanically she lifted one of the 'furniture books' lying in a solemn circle on the table, and was beginning to turn its pages without seeing a word of their contents, when the door opened, and Mildred — a much less smart and imposing Mildred than Sheila had been accustomed to, though she too, in a well-worn alpaca, was very *neat* — came hurrying in.

'Sheila,' she exclaimed, exaggerating the astonishment which was really not so great as she wished it to appear—'Sheila, is it really you? Did you not get my letter, then, after all the trouble I took?'

But just at first, in the delight of finding herself with a friend again, and yielding to a sort of reaction from the restraint she had put upon herself for the last two or three days, Sheila did not take in the very doubtful welcome in Mildred's words and tone. She flung her arms round the other girl's neck, bursting into tears as she did so.

'O Mildred, dearest Mildred,' she said, 'I am so thankful! I thought I should never get here. I have so much to tell you. I have been *so* miserable!'

Mildred was not an ill-natured girl; she was just selfish and shallow. She was very sorry for Sheila, though her uppermost feeling was concern for herself.

'Poor dear,' she said. 'Yes, you had better tell me all at once. Would you mind coming out? There is a quiet corner among the trees, where we should be undisturbed, at the back of the house. I —I am afraid of aunt's coming in. It is just about the time she gets up, and——'

'But haven't you told her I was coming?' said Sheila. 'You must have got my letter yesterday morning. There was no need to make a secret of it.'

'My dear, *you* needn't talk of making secrets of things,' said Mildred, with a little not unnatural acrimony. 'I don't suppose you told your papa and mamma you were going to run away, so I don't see that you need be surprised at my not telling aunt about it. Besides——'

'They *aren't* my father and mother,' said Sheila, with a fresh burst of sobs. 'I've found it all out. I understand now why they've never loved me.'

Mildred looked very startled; she had not expected anything so dramatic as this, for Sheila in her letter had only spoken vaguely and mysteriously. And in spite of her fears of bringing any trouble upon herself, her curiosity was thoroughly aroused. So she spoke more sympathisingly now, though all the same her first idea was to get Sheila safely out of the way.

'Come with me, dear,' she said, passing her arm affectionately through her friend's; 'try to stop crying, do. Come out to my quiet nook. Dear me—what can that be?' she exclaimed, suddenly catching sight of the queerly shaped bundle on a chair. 'What can aunt be thinking of to leave——'

'No, no!' said Sheila, 'it's mine. It's my luggage,' and a half-hysterical laugh escaped her.

This alarmed Mildred still more.

'Hush, hush! do control yourself,' she said, and still holding Sheila's arm she led her out by a glass door at the end of the room, which, small though it was, ran the whole length of the house, into the little garden, which she hurried through, to a sort of tiny orchard beyond. Here in a shady corner was a bench, and there, seating Sheila beside her, she ensconced herself, having taken care to bring the bundle out with them.

'Now, dearest,' she said, 'we shall be *quite* cosy. I am dying to hear all.'

And poor Sheila, choking down her tears — for in a strange way she was beginning to feel almost afraid of Mildred, and not venturing to tell that one cause of her breakdown was that she was faint with hunger, for she had breakfasted very, very early — began her story. It did strike her as she did so that the gypsy's idea of hospitality was a very different one from Mildred's.

It would take too long to relate the conversation. Mildred was extremely interested, but still nothing in Sheila's story tended to lessen her anxiety to keep herself out of trouble. She had sense to know that a young girl's running away from her home was no trifling affair. Even if it were really the case that Sheila was not Mr. and Mrs. Josselin's child, she was pretty certainly their ward — for Mildred had caught up scraps of legal knowledge from her father.

'I do wish you had waited till you heard from me,' she said. 'I wrote at once, no—not to Curlew Moor,' as Sheila started in alarm, 'but under cover to that boy — Conan Sherwood — who is so devoted to you, begging him to find some means of giving you the letter. It would reach him yesterday afternoon. I found out at the post-office, I took heaps of trouble,' in an aggrieved tone, 'and you *said* you would only leave to-day.'

'I know,' said Sheila; 'it was with meeting Diana.'

'That is the worst part of it,' said Mildred. 'Your going about with gypsies does sound so *very* queer, so—so wild and unladylike, you know. I don't know *what* papa and aunt would think of it. It makes me feel even more strongly what I said in my letter.'

'What did you say in your letter?' asked Sheila, in a constrained voice.

'Oh, only that—I begged you to do nothing hasty, and I told you that—you can understand—that I couldn't possibly put you up here.'

'Mildred!' exclaimed Sheila aghast.

'Don't fly off so,' said Mildred. 'I've been thinking that perhaps after all I can make up some kind of story to satisfy aunt. I'll say I met you in the town, as you were on your way to somewhere, and found the trains didn't match, and that I begged you to stay to spend the day, or — I'll manage it somehow,' her secret determination being to tell her father the whole story and get him to take immediate steps for restoring the girl to her legal guardians, by which means she would avoid all blame of herself. 'Though, of course,' she reflected, 'I must not let Sheila suspect this at present, or she would be rushing off, and I might get scolded for letting her go.'

Sheila turned upon her.

'Do you think,' she said, 'that I would agree to such falsehoods? and do you suppose your aunt would believe for an instant that Mr. Josselin's daughter—for I *have* been his daughter—would be allowed to wander about like that alone? You don't understand the way we are brought up.'

Mildred grew red.

'You had better not be rude,' she said. 'I suppose you are beginning to look down upon me now that you see we are not rich or grand. Well, *I* didn't invite you here. And——'

'What?'

'If you are—why, nobody at all—just a waif taken in out of charity, you have no right to give yourself airs.'

'I don't give myself airs, and I don't despise you for being what you are,' said Sheila, coldly furious. 'But I despise you past words for your deceitfulness and meanness, and I wouldn't stay with you if I were dying.'

She stood up as she spoke and caught up her bundle. Mildred grew frightened.

'Where are you going?' she said. 'You know I don't mean to be unkind, but you made me angry, and—and—it is very awkward for me. Where are you going?'

'Back to the railway station,' said Sheila.

Mildred's face cleared.

'Oh, I am glad!' she said. 'You will go straight

home, won't you? It is far the best thing you can do. I am sure they will forgive you, and after all, if they *count* you their daughter, it comes to the same. They will have been so frightened about you that I'm sure they'll be delighted to have you back, trust me.'

'I would rather trust them than you any day,' said Sheila enigmatically.

'There is a train at—let me see. Shall I run in for the railway guide? And—I wonder if I dare go with you to see you off. If it wasn't for that awful bundle—we might go round the long way by the fields without meeting any one. If only I were sure of the trains.'

'Thank you,' said Sheila, 'I will find out at the station.'

And catching sight of a little path round by the side which would doubtless take her through to the street without entering the house, she tossed a contemptuous 'good-bye' to her inhospitable friend and walked off.

CHAPTER IX

LONG AGO

SEVERAL years before the date at which this story begins, Mr. and Mrs. Josselin, with their one child, a baby girl, were living temporarily in London, for though they much preferred the country, Mr. Josselin had no place of his own, and they had not yet decided where their home should be.

It was an interesting subject to discuss, and Mrs. Josselin used to take up the newspaper with eagerness, to see if anything very tempting was to be found among the country houses advertised. One morning—a dark, foggy morning—which made her yearn more than ever to return to the life to which she had always been accustomed, as she was turning the sheet for her usual research, a name on the first column caught her eye. It was her own name: 'Josselin.'

She looked again, and then, addressing her husband at the other side of the breakfast-table, she read the announcement aloud—

'"On the 13th inst., at Joyce de Lyn Court, ——shire, after a short illness, Godfrey, only son of Godfrey Lyn Josselin, Esq., aged twenty-nine." Is that any relation of yours, Arthur?' she inquired.

Mr. Josselin started.

'Dear me,' he said, 'how sad! Relation? Yes, in a sense, though distant. But the ——shire Josselins are the heads of our family, and I fancy that young Godfrey, as we call him, is the last of the branch, unless he has left children. There was some rumour of his marriage a year or two ago, but I never heard it confirmed. I am glad to see he died at home, poor fellow, for his father and he were on very bad terms a while ago.'

'Was he to blame? Was he not satisfactory?'

'Perfectly satisfactory in all essentials, but peculiar, I believe. And his father is proud and tyrannical—the mother died many years ago. Godfrey would not take up politics, and all his tastes were opposed to his father's. He was a great naturalist. The last I heard of him he had broken with his father and gone off to the Rocky Mountains, or somewhere, botanising.'

'How melancholy!' said young Mrs. Josselin. 'Then the old man is all alone?'

'Yes—at least, he had no other children, and no nearer relations on the Josselin side, than ourselves.'

No private intimation of Mr. Godfrey Josselin's death reached his cousin Arthur, however. It was just about this time that he decided on buying Curlew Moor, and in the interest and excitement of all that this involved, both the young husband and wife almost forgot the few sad lines which had caught their attention. For the cousins had scarcely ever met; and a letter with a deep black border, which reached Mr. Arthur Josselin a month or two after the morning I have told you of, astonished him not a little.

'Evelyn,' he said to his wife, looking up gravely, after reading it, 'I am very sorry,' for they had planned to go down that very day to see about some improvements in their new house; 'I fear I must leave you for a day or two. This is a most unexpected summons, but one which must be obeyed.'

The letter was from the doctor in attendance at Joyce de Lyn Court. He wrote at the request of old Mr. Josselin, whom he described as most seriously ill, and not likely to live many days, to beg Mr. Arthur Josselin to go to his cousin at once, as the dying man had some important matters to speak to him about, as his nearest relation.

'It will be an act of real kindness,' added the writer on his own account, 'to come at once. My patient has never recovered from the shock of his son's death. He is very sad and lonely.'

'Yes,' Mrs. Josselin agreed, 'you must go. I hope,' she added, 'it is not to tell you that you are his heir; we are quite rich enough, and I should never like that far-off county as much as dear Curlew, which I have learnt to love already.'

Mr. Josselin smiled. He felt the same as his wife.

He was away nearly a week, and when he returned he looked worn and tired. It had been a melancholy visit. Mr. Josselin had died two days after his cousin reached him.

'Evelyn,' he said, after he had told her the first few details of his time at Joyce de Lyn, 'I do not know what you will say to me when I tell you what I have promised—what I have undertaken in your name. It seemed to me I had no choice.'

Mrs. Josselin looked up in alarm.

'Oh, not that we are to go to live up there, in that great, gloomy place!' she exclaimed.

'No,' he replied, 'not that,' and her face cleared. 'It is something quite different. I have accepted, for us both, the guardianship of a little girl, and under very peculiar conditions. She is a very dear little thing, and I have promised that she shall be to us absolutely as our own child. There is about a year between her and our little girl, and they must believe themselves to be sisters.'

Mrs. Josselin looked perplexed.

'Dear Arthur,' she said, 'I am *quite* ready—happy to take the child, but—is it wise to hide the truth? I do not like concealment. I am sure we can love her just as much if she knows, and our own child knows, that she is not really our daughter.'

Then he explained. It was a long and complicated story. I will tell it as shortly as I can.

The quarrel between old Mr. Josselin and his son had ended, as we know, in Godfrey going away to America. But he did not go alone. He married, just before sailing, a sweet and good girl to whom he had been attached for some time. She was beneath him in rank, for her father was only the bailiff of a property in the next county, and for long her family refused to let her marry young Mr. Josselin for fear of his father's displeasure. But when they found that the old man had cast him off for other reasons —indeed, Mr. Josselin had never heard of Lettice Flower—and Godfrey told them he was going to make his home in America, they gave in. The Flowers themselves were at that time emigrating to Canada, so they all went together. Godfrey had a few happy years—the happiest he had ever known —then poor Lettice died, very soon after her little girl was born, leaving her husband broken-hearted. A few months later he received one day, to his great surprise, a letter from his father. The old man had been very ill and his heart had softened to his son. Godfrey replied at once, telling of his marriage, the birth of his little daughter, his wife's death and his own sadness. And this letter drew forth another begging him to return to England at once.

'Bring the child with you,' wrote the old man; 'I do not want to hear anything about her relations on the other side. She shall belong to you and me alone. I am pleased that you have given her for one of her names that of our ancestress, Lady Sheila.'

Now Godfrey was much and deeply attached to

his wife's family, and his father's tone about them made him so angry that he was on the point of writing off to decline the proposal altogether. But the Flowers begged him not to do so. Some day, they said, Mr. Josselin might come to know them better; and after all, he was Godfrey's father, an old and lonely man. For the baby's sake, too, the offer should be accepted. And the parting, they hoped, would not be for very long, as they had thoughts of returning to England again themselves, having started their two younger sons in a farm where they were doing well.

'Father and I are getting old,' said Mrs. Flower, 'and if George gets the chance a few years hence of Lord Lexing's other place, as is promised him when it falls vacant, we could all settle down in the old country again, for Mary is like our own daughter.'

'Mary' was George Flower's wife. They had two children, a little older than Godfrey Josselin's daughter.

Godfrey took their advice and started for England. But sorrow and trouble had done him more harm than was suspected. He caught cold on the voyage, neglected it, and only lived a fortnight after his return to his own old home, leaving his tiny daughter to his father's care. He was not able to say much about his wife's relations before he died, for Mr. Josselin was still violent and obstinate, and any attempt to argue away his prejudices was sure to lead to angry discussion, for which poor Godfrey was in no fit state.

Some weeks passed. The grandfather was devoted to the baby girl, and for a time it seemed as if the interest of this innocent fresh life was going to prolong his own. But it was not to be. There came another stroke of paralysis, from which he did not rally as before; then worse symptoms, and at last the certainty that death was near. And in his extremity he sent for his relation, Arthur Josselin, whom he knew to be a high-principled man, with a good and charming wife. To him he made the request which, on his return to London, Mr. Arthur Josselin told Mrs. Josselin of.

But here I must explain that the whole facts of the case were not known to Mr. Arthur Josselin as I have here related them. He knew nothing of the Flowers except from his old kinsman, and he, of course, was full of prejudice against them. Had it been otherwise it is not probable that the younger man would have agreed to the strange conditions added to his guardianship—conditions which, as we have seen, Mrs. Josselin dreaded and disliked from the first.

'Are you sure,' she said to her husband when he had finished speaking—' are you sure old Mr. Josselin was not unreasonably prejudiced against poor Godfrey's wife and her family?'

Mr. Arthur Josselin looked distressed.

'Very possibly,' he said. 'I suppose the truth is, he knew very little about them. He said openly he would not let Godfrey mention them. But I seemed to have no choice—he was dying; and, after all, the secret is only to be kept for a few years—till the child is twelve. He wanted her, he said, to be thoroughly *Josselin* in affections and associations, before she learns the truth of her own position. For she will be very, very rich, you see, Evelyn, and might fall a prey to the graspingness of those relations, if they had anything to do with her.'

'But so far away as they are—in Canada!' said Mrs. Josselin.

'They are returning to this country, unfortunately. Godfrey told his father so, and it increased the old man's fears. Rightly or wrongly, he was perfectly sure they meant to try to get hold of the child somehow.'

'But they *could* not if you are her guardian.'

'No, very true. But still it might be disagreeable, and worse, if they are underhand, designing people. A curious little incident which happened a few weeks ago added to the old man's fears, though I daresay he was nervous and fanciful. You know Joyce Court—they drop the "de Lyn" up there, it makes such a mouthful of the name—is quite among the moors, a lonely, wild country, and rather a haunt of gypsies. Well, an old gypsy presented herself at the house not long ago, demanding to see Mr. Godfrey. She had brought him news, she said, from over the water. When told of his death, she fell into great grief and begged to see the child. But this Mr. Josselin would not hear of. I fancy he was very rough to the woman, but they had hard work to get rid of her. And he was firmly convinced she had come to steal the baby. "Her mother may have been a gypsy herself for all I know," he said to me, half mockingly; but that, of course, was nonsense. He had all the particulars of Godfrey's marriage from the poor fellow before he died.'

Mrs. Josselin was silent.

'And, you see,' her husband went on, 'all seemed to fit in. We are just going to live at a new place, where no one will be surprised at our having two children instead of one. Our servants will all be new, except Ellen, and she, I think, we must confide in.'

'Yes,' said Mrs. Josselin, though reluctantly. 'It does seem quite possible. I certainly could not do it *without* Ellen; it is curious that even my maid is leaving to-morrow to be married; and the new one only comes next week.'

'I have planned it all,' Mr. Josselin went on. 'The child's nurse will bring her up to London on Monday, and Ellen shall go with me to the station to fetch her. We shall at once go down to Brighton for a few days, you and our baby meeting us there—if you can manage the journey with her alone?'

'Oh yes,' Mrs. Josselin replied; 'she is growing so big and sensible now.'

'At Brighton,' he went on, 'you must engage an under-nurse—Ellen could not manage both—and by then Curlew will be nearly ready for us.'

All took place as proposed. The little stranger was soon quite at home among her new friends, and from the first day of her coming to them no shadow of difference was made by Mr. and Mrs. Josselin between her and their own little daughter.

There was one small difficulty. Both children

were 'Sheila,' and hitherto this name had been used for both, though both had another as well. So for one of them the second name had to be adopted, and thus 'Sheila Margaret' and 'Sheila Honor' came to be 'Sheila' and 'Honor.'

A few, but very few, of Mr. and Mrs. Josselin's nearest relations had to be confided in. But he and she were both 'only' children, so this did not cause much difficulty. And though Mrs. Josselin never ceased to long for the day when everything might be openly known, all promised well and happily. There was only one crook in the lot, one sad thorn of trouble, which began to make itself felt even in the children's infancy. This was the violent and jealous temper of the elder of the two little girls—'Sheila.'

Before returning to her whom all this time we have left starting off, in her indignation at Mildred's conduct, to the railway station at Hexford, thence to travel she knew not where, it may be well to explain in what way old Diana had been connected with Mr. Godfrey Josselin's life in Canada.

You remember that the Flower family all travelled over together to Canada, with their married daughter and her husband. In the same steamer, among the poor steerage passengers, was a woman, aged even then, twelve or thirteen years before we first come across her in this story as *very* old. Steerage passengers are often a rough lot, and this poor thing became a sort of butt for their rude jokes. For she was a gypsy, a woman of great importance among her own people, not accustomed to be mocked or jeered at. It is not often that gypsies are met with travelling across the Atlantic, and the reason of Diana's journey was a touching one. A favourite grandson of hers had got into trouble for stealing. He had been convicted and imprisoned. When his time was over, he was too proud to return, disgraced, to his tribe, and he accepted the offer of some benevolent society to help him to emigrate. This had happened three years before. Since then 'Johnny' had done well; but he yearned for the sight of a familiar face. He managed to save enough to pay half his granny's fare, she finding the rest, and off came the brave old woman.

Some little accident made Godfrey and his brother-in-law, George Flower, acquainted with the cruel treatment the gypsy was exposed to on board the steamer. They interfered to protect her, and, by paying something extra, got her into more comfortable quarters on board. Then when they reached the other side, finding that her 'boy,' a man of five-and-twenty by now, was living not very far from their new home, they helped her on her journey and made her come to them for a while before she went back to England. Her gratitude was deep.

Three or four years later, she came again, bringing with her this time a girl for Johnny to marry, for he could not make up his mind to any but a gypsy wife. And again she visited her kind friends, to find them, alas! in sad trouble—Lettice dead, Godfrey and his baby daughter off to England, sore fears in their hearts that the proud grandfather might do his best to prevent their ever seeing the child again. For 'rather than make bad blood between Godfrey and his father,' said old Mrs. Flower, who had come to consider Diana quite a friend, 'we'd keep ourselves out of the way altogether.'

But the gypsy cheered her up. They were soon returning to England. Mr. Godfrey had a true heart. And in her own mind she resolved to take the first chance of being near Joyce Court, in order to see Godfrey and tell him how his wife's relations yearned after the child. Here was a service she could render to her benefactors.

We have heard how her visit to Godfrey's home turned out.

But she was a determined old woman.

After the old man's death, she found out that the child had been sent away to some of his relations. It was she who first told the Flowers, who came to England a few years later, where the child was, though she had great difficulty in discovering this. And from time to time she visited her old friends in their new home at Lexing, and the talk was always of 'Lettice's baby.'

'But so long as she is happy and well,' said the Flowers, 'we will not interfere. It is right that she should be brought up in her own position in life.'

At long intervals during those years, Diana managed to visit the neighbourhood of Curlew Moor. But though not *very* far from Lexing, it was not a part of the country frequented by gypsies, and she was afraid of attracting notice if she alone, or with her 'children,' were seen there often. She succeeded, however, in finding out that Mr. and Mrs. Josselin were well spoken of as kind and generous, and for some time she was able to tell her friends at Lexing that Lettice's daughter seemed in good hands. She never was fortunate enough to see the Josselin children. They were carefully guarded, more so than they realised, or than is usual, for Mr. Josselin had not forgotten his old relation's warnings against his little grand-daughter's mother's family. But on one of her visits some gossip reached Diana's ears of troubles at the 'big hoose'—a young servant had brought home to the village, chatter about Miss Sheila's 'awful temper,' and her not 'getting on' with her parents and sister. At once the gypsy was on the alert. The name 'Sheila' made her certain that the child spoken of was the one she was interested in, and her quick imagination at once decided that the time for interference was at hand.

'They are beginning to ill-treat her; they think she has no one to defend her,' she said to herself. 'They shall find they are mistaken.'

She hung about the place for a day or two, in hopes of some lucky chance throwing the young girl in her way, before the gypsies set off again on the round which, after a while, would bring her near the Flowers' home, when she could consult them. And we know what came of her hiding in the haunted wood, and how the sight of Sheila's unhappiness made her resolve to help her in running away. And now it is time to return to Hexford.

CHAPTER X

'YOU ARE NOT LIKE YOUR MOTHER'

SHEILA'S indignation against Mildred—better justified than her anger often was, and all the deeper because her self-respect made her keep an outward appearance of calm—helped her to retrace her steps coolly enough to the station. And though one or two passers-by glanced back with surprise at the refined and ladylike girl, evidently a stranger in the place, carrying a bundle like a dressmaker's apprentice, nobody took much notice of her.

But when she got to the railway, and sat down in the empty waiting-room, her heart began to fail her. She had allowed Mildred to think, or to *pretend* to think (for in reality I doubt if the girl was as sure of it as she would have maintained), that she was going home again, for she would have done almost anything rather than remain even an hour or two under Miss Frost's inhospitable roof; but she was still far from dreaming of such a thing as a return to Curlew Moor. She *wished* she could; the trials and miseries, as she had thought them, of her life there were rapidly growing smaller and fainter as she thought them over. On the whole, she was beginning to say to herself that it was wonderful that she should have received the care and kindness that had been hers all the years she could remember—she, 'a waif,' belonging to nobody, as Mildred had called her! She had learned some bitter lessons during her short interview with the girl she had thought her friend.

'Only they did not love me; they could not, I suppose. I am ill-tempered and unlovable by nature. It would have been truer kindness to have left me wherever I was than to bring me up without telling me the truth, and without loving me. *Perhaps* if I had known the truth I should have been grateful, and that might have made me nicer. I don't know——'

But one thing was certain, she could not and would not go back. It would be too terrible, too trying, to know that she had no right to be there; that the only feeling they *could* have to her now would be pity, for less than ever was there any chance of her winning affection. And the idea of being sent off to school in disgrace, as no doubt she would be, was not to be thought of for a moment.

But where should she go? She could not go back to Diana—two days of that life was as much as she could have borne; besides, she had no claim on the poor old gypsy, no right to live upon *her*. The thought of Diana, however, brought something else to her mind. What was it that her strange friend had asked her to remember? What were the names she had made her repeat? Sheila had a good memory, and they soon came back to her—'Mr. Flower, Moorecroft Farm, near Lexing.'

Yes, that was it.

But who could Mr. Flower be? Sheila had never heard of him before, she was sure.

'Most likely,' she thought, it's just somebody who's been kind to the gypsies, and of course Diana doesn't understand that for me it would be quite different.' But still—Diana was not at all stupid. Perhaps she did understand better than seemed likely.

'At any rate,' Sheila went on in her own mind, 'she was right about Mildred. She knew somehow that *she* was not to be counted upon, and certainly I have more reason to trust poor Diana than *her*.

Possibly this Mr. Flower has a kind wife or daughter, and they might take me in for a few days till I can think what is best to do. I have got some money still—I could pay for a room. My travelling hasn't cost me much so far.'

She took out her purse. There still remained one pound, fifteen shillings, and a few coppers.

'I will ask the fare to Lexing and how long it takes to get there. That can do no harm anyway,' she decided.

'Lexing,' repeated the clerk at the ticket window. He happened to be rather a good-natured young man and had nothing particular to do just then. 'Lexing—well, it's no distance if you catch a train at the junction, but it's on a different line, and there's only two trains in the day that fit. One's just gone, and the other good one doesn't pass this till five in the evening.'

'Five in the evening!' repeated Sheila in dismay.

'You can get as far as Barford by the 12.45 from this,' said the obliging clerk. 'That's the junction. You'd have an hour to wait there, but even with that you'd get to Lexing before three.'

'I'll do that,' said Sheila, who had a nervous fear of Mildred's coming or sending after her. 'What o'clock is it now? And what's the fare to Lexing, please?'

The man twisted his head round as if he wanted to try how far it would go without coming off. It was only to see the clock and save himself the trouble of moving.

'Twelve thirty-seven,' he replied. 'Second-class?'

'I'm not sure,' said Sheila, to whom the possibility of third-class had presented itself for the first time. 'How much is it, please? And — how much is third?'

She was only a little more than twelve years old. But she was tall. It never occurred to the man that she was under age, and this rather pleased her.

'Third-class, seven and eightpence,' he replied. 'Second, ten and ninepence.'

Sheila was learning to calculate her resources. If Moorecroft were some way from Lexing, she might have to pay for a fly, and she was very anxious to keep her one gold piece untouched. She had no idea how much a fly might cost. It was best to be prudent, so she decided on a third-class ticket.

It was not so bad as she had feared. All the way to Barford she was alone in the compartment. But

Barford Station was rather bustling and crowded. It was market-day there, and already some of the quick and energetic folk were returning to their homes. Sheila by this time was faint with hunger, but she was so nervously afraid of missing the train on to Lexing that, though she had an hour to wait, she dared not leave the station. To her delight, however, she spied a small stall set out with cakes and oranges and gingerbeer a few yards outside the gates, and there she spent sixpence on some very stale buns and very frothy gingerbeer, both of which tasted excellent, thanks to the sauce with which they were flavoured. Then she found a bench near to the side of the platform from which the train for Lexing started, and sat there for the rest of the time waiting patiently.

All her hopes were now centred on Moorecroft and 'Mr. Flower.' If they failed her, she could not have said what she meant to do. But at such times the mind often refuses to look further. One should be grateful that it is so.

There were a great many people, nearly all third-class passengers, waiting for the train, and when it at last came up, Sheila had to fight her way through a crowd of basket-laden country-women, and hot, red-faced men, before she could get a seat in any of the overflowing carriages. And when at last she found herself landed in one, it was only standing-room that at first offered itself. She was one too many.

But there was no time to get out and look for a less crowded compartment; the train was just moving.

'Never mind, lovey,' said a fat woman whose baskets took up as much room as herself, 'I'll be getting out at t'next stopping, and then you can set you down.'

Sheila thanked her, but the little conversation had caught the ears of a middle-aged man with a quiet, plain face, who had just opened out a newspaper and was preparing to enjoy it in a corner. He looked up, and, taking in the situation at a glance, rose from his place.

'Take my seat, miss,' he said. 'It'll not be for long.'

'Thank you very much,' she replied gratefully, and something in the refined tone of voice made the man—a better-class farmer he looked—glance at her again. But he said no more, and soon he was absorbed in the newspaper, which he managed to read standing.

The train pulled up in about a quarter of an hour. Out got the fat woman and the baskets, and a couple of others not quite so fat, and not quite so basket-ridden. At the next stoppage two or three men followed their example, and this went on, till at the last halt before Lexing only one passenger remained besides Sheila's middle-aged friend and herself. This man was evidently an acquaintance of the quiet-faced farmer, as they had exchanged a few remarks, and as he prepared to get out, Sheila overheard him add, as he bade the other 'good-day,' 'All well at Moorecroft, I hope?'

'Yes, thank you,' said the farmer, then the train grunted on again, and again her companion relapsed into his paper.

But Sheila was making up her mind to something. She looked at his face: it was both firm and gentle —a face one could trust. It almost reminded her— though Mr. Josselin was very handsome and high-bred in appearance, and this man was plain — of 'papa.' And at the thought that he was no longer 'papa,' the hot tears filled her eyes. She brushed them away, however, and then, waiting a moment, to be sure that her voice was quite steady, she began, with a timidity new to her, to speak.

'If you please,' she said, 'can you tell me—did not the—the person who got out just now say something about Moorecroft? Can you tell me where Moorecroft is?'

The farmer looked at her in great surprise.

'Certainly I can, my dear,' he said, for he now saw how very young she was. 'It is my home.'

'Then are you Mr. Flower?' she asked eagerly. 'Oh, I am so glad! I was going to Moorecroft. I wanted to know if I could stay there a day or two—till—till——'

Mr. Flower was completely bewildered. Then it suddenly occurred to him that perhaps the young girl was a friend or relation of a lady, an old acquaintance of his wife's, who had sometimes spent a few weeks with them in the summer.

'Are you a friend—a niece, perhaps—of Mrs. Clarkson's?' he inquired. 'What is your name?'

'Sheila Josselin,' she replied hastily, then suddenly growing scarlet. 'No, no,' she went on, 'that's a mistake; please forget I said it. My name is Robin—Margaret Robin.'

But it was too late. The second name might have been unuttered, it made no impression whatever on the hearer. His sunburnt face became strangely pale.

'Sheila Josselin,' he repeated. 'Lettice's baby; Lettice's little girl at last. Yet—can it be? So unlike——'

But he quickly recovered himself.

'Tell me all about yourself, my child,' he said. 'Who told you of us? Who sent you to us? And why did you leave your—your home?'

'The gypsy—Diana—told me to go to you if I was in difficulty,' said Sheila, nearly as surprised as he. 'She said you would be very kind.'

'But still,' he exclaimed, 'I do not understand. Diana, poor old Diana! I hope she has done nothing wrong. She did not lead you away from your home, I trust? You were happy there, we thought.'

Sheila hesitated. Her mind and nerves had gone through so much in the last few days that she did not seem to have the usual power of grasping things quickly. For a moment or two it did not strike her as extraordinary that this Mr. Flower, this complete stranger, should know so much about her. But his words about 'home' brought back a flood of bitterness.

'I—I thought I wasn't happy there. I think now it was mostly my own fault,' she said. 'But I can never go back—never. They don't love me, and

'Sheila Josselin,' he repeated. 'Lettice's baby; Lettice's little girl at last. —P. 158.

now I know why. I daresay they tried to love me, and I must have seemed horrible—ungrateful and horrid. But I didn't know, and oh, I do think it was wrong to deceive me!'

She scarcely realised whom she was speaking to, or indeed that she was speaking to any one. But Mr. Flower seemed to require no explanation of her words.

'You did not know?' he said. 'You have always thought you were their child.'

'Of course I did, though I have often thought they didn't love me so much as my sister—no,' with a sudden rush of tears to her eyes, 'she's not my sister. And she does love me, and I love her. Oh yes, I love them all, though I don't wonder they couldn't believe it.'

Mr. Flower looked very grave—very sad too. But he did not answer at once. Instead of doing so he took out his watch—a plain silver one, attached to a silver chain—and looked at it.

'We have twenty minutes still to Lexing,' he said; 'the train does not stop now. Tell me all you can, my dear, and then we shall see.'

Something in her new friend's manner, plain and homely as he was, inspired Sheila with confidence.

She was beginning, too, to realise by this time that he must have some peculiar knowledge of her history. So she did as he asked, and told him all, though it was not without great effort over herself that she kept back the tears that almost choked her.

Mr. Flower listened, scarcely interrupting her by word or gesture. Then he said gravely—

'We are close to Lexing now. Moorecroft is two miles from there. My dogcart will meet me at the station, and I will take you home with me. It is the best thing—the only thing to be done in the meantime. But I must talk all over with—with your grandmother and your aunt, before I can say much.'

Sheila stopped crying in her amazement.

'My grandmother,' she exclaimed, 'and my aunt! Both my grandmothers are dead, and I haven't any aunts.'

Mr. Flower looked at her, and on his grave face there appeared the glimmer of a smile.

'Yes, my dear,' he said. 'You forget that you are not the daughter of Mr. Arthur Josselin and his wife, kind though I must say they have been to you. Your grandmother is my mother, your aunt is my wife. For though your name *is* Sheila Josselin, your mother was my sister—Lettice Flower.'

Sheila grew very, very pale. Somehow, till now, a sort of wild hope had still lingered at the bottom of her heart that she was going to find that after all there had been some dreadful mistake, that she *was* herself, that 'papa and mamma' were what they had always been. But this quiet matter-of-fact statement put to flight every dream. She could see and feel for herself that George Flower was not the sort of person to say a thing he was not sure of. And for a moment or two she gasped for breath, looking almost as if she were going to faint.

Mr. Flower was very sorry for her.

'It is hard upon you,' he said. 'I cannot understand why it has been concealed. It is that that has done all the mischief. Heaven knows,' he went on, as if speaking to himself, 'we would not have interfered if it had been better for the child.'

By degrees Sheila recovered herself a little. She looked up.

'Then how am I Sheila Josselin?' she said. 'I can't understand anything. Won't you explain? And how did Diana know?'

'I will tell you all I can on the way to Moore-

M

croft,' he replied, for the train was already slackening to stop. 'I do not myself understand the secrecy—it is inconsistent with Arthur Josselin's character.'

And during the three miles' drive he told her the whole story which we already know. He told it carefully and precisely, allowing no personal feeling to colour his view, for he was a very just man. And Sheila listened and did her best to take it calmly and reasonably. But the agony in her heart was great.

'Why did they keep it a secret?' she said. '*Perhaps* if I had known it, I might have been a better girl. For I see now how very, very trying I have been—full of ill-temper and jealousy—and to-day, what Mildred said about my being a waif, belonging to nobody, and that they picked me up out of pity—oh, it was horrible!' and she shuddered at the remembrance.

Mr. Flower started, and for the first time a dark flush rose in his face, and he muttered something to himself not too complimentary to Miss Frost.

'Well, *that* at least is not the case,' he said. 'Godfrey Josselin's child is no waif or stray, or pauper either, for that matter. Keep up your heart, my dear. You will never be the worse for seeing your own faults. And maybe all this trouble has been sent for your good. That's what granny will have to say about it, and mother too, you'll see; for here we are at home.'

'Home' was a rather picturesque farmhouse. For though George Flower was the bailiff of Lord Lexing's ——shire property, he did a little farming on his own account too—it was an amusement to his old father, he used to say, and granny would have been lost without a bit of a dairy and a poultry-yard. But the picturesqueness was only outside. Indoors, though very neat and exquisitely clean, it was very, very plain. There was no pretence of aping 'gentry' about the Flowers. And when her new friend exclaimed, as they were driving up to the door, 'There's mother—that's your aunt, Sheila,' the girl, in spite of all, had some difficulty in overcoming the strange sensation of disappointment at perceiving how very homely a person 'Aunt' was, pleasant and sensible though her face seemed. 'How astonished she'll be!' added George Flower.

But for once he was mistaken. Mrs. George Flower looked eager and excited, but not so amazed as he expected.

'Have you met her, then?' she exclaimed, hurrying forward and shading her eyes from the evening sun. 'How did you manage that? My dear child, my poor dear, let me help you down. Welcome to Moorecroft—welcome home, my love.'

And a good hearty kiss followed her cordial words, a kiss which Sheila wished she could have felt more grateful for. But fortunately the husband and wife were too busy in explaining things to each other to notice the pale, cold misery looking out of Sheila's face. 'Home,' she repeated to herself.

'How did I know?' Mary Flower was saying, when Sheila caught the sense of her words. 'Why, who do you think has been here? One of old Diana's lads, with a letter from her—a queer letter, as you can fancy—saying that we were to lose no time in fetching this dear child home. I've been on thorns till you came, meaning to send you straight back to Hexford, to the house the boy told us of.'

A light broke on Sheila, and a little colour came into her face.

'Oh!' she exclaimed, 'that must have been the dark gypsy-looking boy who offered to carry my bundle. How stupid of me not to think of it before!'

Mary Flower turned to her eagerly and made her relate it all. Then she said anxiously—

'She's near dead with tiredness, and hungry too, I'll be bound. We'll have tea in a minute. And there's granny all in a tremble with the news the boy brought. You'll have to see granny first of anything, Sheila.'

And Sheila, feeling again as if she were in some strange dream, found herself led into the large, bare farm-kitchen, where, near the fire, on a rocking-chair, sat an old white-haired woman, with a sweet face and wistful eyes.

'She's come, granny,' said George Flower's wife. 'They met in the train, just fancy!' and she pushed Sheila forward as she spoke.

Old Mrs. Flower drew the girl's face down towards her own and kissed her softly.

'Lettice's baby,' she murmured. Then she gently moved the girl a little from her, as if for a better view. 'My dear,' she said, 'you have a look—is it of your father?—though he was a brown-haired man, and none so dark-eyed as you—yet still you have a look. But you're not like your mother.'

Nevertheless she kissed her again, and from that moment Sheila felt more at home with granny than with any one else at Moorecroft.

CHAPTER XI

A STRANGER AT CURLEW MOOR

CONSIDERING everything, it was scarcely to be wondered at that the next morning found Sheila so utterly tired out that she was obliged to stay in bed. The excitement of all her conflicting feelings had kept her up hitherto, but now that she was, in a sense, at rest, she seemed to collapse.

Her new friends were distressed and rather anxious. They had welcomed her so heartily that it was disappointing to find her so sad and crushed-looking.

'I can't make her out,' said Bessie, Mr. and Mrs. George Flower's daughter, a hearty, sensible sort of girl, with something of her Aunt Lettice's fair beauty about her. 'If she's been so miserable with those stuck-up Josselins that she actually ran away, she should be glad to be with her own folk, and not sit there staring with those big dark eyes, as if she was too miserable to say a word.'

'She's just tired out, poor dear,' said granny, who never had a harsh thought of any one, though in her heart she too was perplexed and disappointed.

This was later in the evening of Sheila's arrival. She had gone to bed, owning herself very tired, after doing her best to eat some of the cold meat and apple pie which had been set out on the kitchen table for supper. But she was not hungry now, and the plainness and homeliness of everything—the steel-pronged forks, and rather coarse, though clean, table-cloth— repelled her in a way she was ashamed of. She had never before known how fastidious and dainty she was, and she had none of the bright readiness to be pleased with everything which would have made little Honor at home in no time with the good Flowers.

So Bessie took her upstairs to bed—to the room she was to share with her—a plain room, like everything else in the house, with two small beds and ordinary painted furniture, no carpet on the well-scrubbed floor except a strip or two of faded drugget, no curtains to the windows, and an old-fashioned paper—vine leaves in trellis-work—on the walls, yet a room which Bessie evidently regarded with great pride.

The two beds were handy in the summer, when they now and then had 'visitors' for a little, she explained—meaning boarders—for the family had to work hard, and of late Bessie's brother's schooling had been expensive, for Jack was a clever boy and getting a good education, she told Sheila. And she would have sat down there and then for a good chat, if her newly-found cousin had shown the slightest inclination for anything of the kind. But a weary 'Yes, please,' or 'No, thank you,' was all she could extract, and poor Bessie was really feeling very puzzled and a little hurt when she joined the grown-up people again downstairs in the kitchen.

George Flower heard what his mother and daughter said without speaking for a minute or two. Then he looked up.

'I'd best tell you all she's told me,' he began. 'There's two sides to most things, and I want to be fair. I must say I can't see that the child's relations have behaved unkindly to her. There's only one thing I can blame them for. But I'm afraid Sheila herself is queer-tempered and jealous. She's owned as much to me, and she's sorry for it—very sorry.

I'm afraid it's all been temper more than actual grounds for complaint, and I'm really at a loss to say what we should do.'

Then he went on to give more in detail all that Sheila had told him—her conviction that 'nobody loved her,' her growing consciousness of her own jealous and selfish character, her misery at the discovery she had made.

'If it wasn't for that,' she had said, 'I'd go back now and tell them how sorry I am, and ask them to forgive me. But I do think *that* was hard on me. Why was it kept a secret?'

'And that's what I can't make out myself,' said George Flower.

'They seem to be taking her leaving home pretty coolly,' said his wife, who was reluctant to give up the idea that Sheila had been cruelly treated, and had run off to her own people for protection.

'How can we say that?' said George quickly. 'They know nothing of us—they know that the child had never heard of us. There was no reason to think they'd send here. But I'll tell you what's growing clearer and plainer to me every minute. I must go to them—I must see Arthur Josselin, and tell him she's safe here, and have it all out with him.

By all accounts—poor Godfrey always spoke well of him—this Mr. Josselin's an honest and honourable man, and we must behave fair to him. And after all, when all's said and done, he's the child's legal guardian.'

There was silence for a moment or two. Then old Mr. Flower spoke up in his rather tremulous voice—

'Yes, my lad,' he said, 'I think you're right. You'd best start as soon as you can. Take the first train in the morning, and maybe you can be back again at night. We don't want to act underhandedly in any way. If Lettice's child could be happy with us, we'd be only too happy to have her. But—I misdoubt me if it would do. She's been brought up in different ways. Still, you can say it, and be sure to say too, we'd want no money with her. What there is for her—and I suppose there'll be something, though we were told the property was to go to these other Josselins—had best be saved till she's grown up.'

'I'll put it as you wish, father,' replied George. 'But about the money—I don't know, I'm sure, how Sheila comes in, in that way. Maybe'—for some vague ideas were beginning to shape themselves in his rather slow but wise head which might help to explain things—'maybe there's been some things not rightly understood in that way too. Anyhow, I'll be plain-spoken and straightforward, and if Arthur Josselin's what I think, he'll be the same with me.'

He was off the next morning before Sheila was awake, or at least before Bessie came down with her rather disappointing report of their visitor's feeling so ill.

But Mrs. George Flower's heart was in the right place, as people say. She was upstairs in Sheila's room in no time, condoling with her and comforting her. It was only a wonder she was no worse, considering all she'd gone through, poor dear. A day or two would see her all right again, and meantime she mustn't think of getting up or doing anything but rest. Granny would like nothing better than to come up and sit beside her with her knitting, and talk about long ago, when Sheila's mother, sweet Lettice, was a girl at home.

They were very, very good to her, and Sheila was grateful and tried to show it. To old Mrs. Flower she found it easier to talk than to Bessie and her mother. She wanted to be affectionate to them, but their very heartiness repelled her. They were so good and simple, but they did not understand her, and even while feeling disgusted with herself for it, she shivered at the idea of spending her life with them. The gentle grandmother suited her better just because she *was* so gentle, wise with the experience of a long life, sympathising, and naturally refined, though, like the rest of the family, entirely without pretension. Sheila learnt more than she knew during the few days she was obliged to stay in bed, with granny sitting knitting beside her, and granny got to love the girl for her own sake, and to discern the underlying good in Sheila's character.

Mr. George Flower did not return home the same night, as he intended. On the contrary, the next morning brought a letter from him written at Curlew Moor, bidding his wife not to expect him till the following day. And here, perhaps, it may be well to relate what happened to him on his journey to Sheila's home.

The railway station, as we know, was at some little distance from Mr. Josselin's house. But it was still early when Mr. Flower got out of the train, for he had started almost at daybreak, and he decided to walk to Curlew. A man whom he met on the road showed him a short cut through the fields, adding that it would bring him into the grounds by a side way.

'You won't have to pass the lodge,' he added. 'That would be much farther round,' and then it seemed to Mr. Flower that the man looked at him rather curiously, as if on the point of saying something more. The idea was correct, for his informant was an under-gardener at Mr. Josselin's, well aware, like every one about the place, of the miserable anxiety the family was in about the disappearance of the elder child. And it was on Smithson's tongue to ask if possibly the stranger were the bearer of any news. But George Flower had no intention of disclosing his business to any chance passer-by, so with a rather curt 'Thank you,' he walked on, Smithson standing still and looking after him.

'A detective in plain clothes, I'll lay anything,' he said to himself, greatly pleased at his own sagacity. 'They say as how them there fellows get themselves up to look what they like, but I'm not so easy caught. There's something about that one different from what he seems.'

So there was. The same quiet dignity which had won Sheila's confidence made itself felt in George Flower by all with whom he came in contact.

He walked on some way farther, skirting the wood where, not yet a week ago, old Diana had met Sheila for the first time; then a turn to the right took him down a short lane, to a gate whence a second drive led to the house.

But to-day, for some reason or other, this gate was padlocked. Somewhat annoyed, for he did not want to retrace his steps all the way to the high road, Mr. Flower was just thinking whether it would be well to climb over, when he caught sight of a small figure coming towards him down the drive. It was a boy, and he walked slowly, for he was lame, and as he came quite near, the stranger saw that the child's face was pale and his eyes red, as if he had been crying.

The farmer's kind heart felt sorry for him. He wondered who he was, for he was sure Mr. Josselin had no son; yet this boy was unmistakably a gentleman, and he seemed in trouble.

'Can you kindly tell me how I can get to the house without a long round?' he said. 'I was directed this way, but the gate is padlocked.'

'Is it?' said the boy. 'It isn't usually—but it doesn't matter. If you go back to the wood you'll find a path leading straight to the house, or, if you don't mind, there's a gap between the hedge and the wall a few yards to the left. I *think* you could get through. I must get out that way myself. I didn't know the gate was locked.'

But he eyed Mr. Flower's large frame doubtfully.

'No,' he said, 'you'd better go by the wood. I'll come round to you and show you the way.'

He turned back again in among the shrubs, and in a few moments the stranger heard the tap of his approaching crutch on the ground. A new idea had struck the boy.

'Do you mind telling me,' he said courteously, but without any timidity, 'if you want to see Mr. Josselin, and if it's about anything particular? They're—they are in great trouble at the house,' and the tears rushed to his eyes.

George Flower laid his hand on the boy's shoulder.

'I know they must be,' he said ; 'are you one of them?'

'No, oh no!' said Con, 'I'm only a friend, but I'm awfully unhappy, for I'm very fond of her. And mother thinks I've been to blame. *They* don't,' with a jerk of his head towards the invisible house; 'but——' he broke off abruptly, 'I'm talking as if you knew all about it. Do you—oh, have you by any chance brought news of her—of Sheila?'

Mr. Flower was far too kind to beat about the bush.

'Yes,' he said directly, 'the best news. Sheila is safe and well in my house—near Lexing—she found her way to us yesterday.'

The revulsion of feeling was too much for delicate, sensitive Con. He sat down on the grass bordering the lane and burst into tears. George let him cry for a moment or two, then he said quietly—

'I have a good deal to say to Mr. Josselin. Do you think I shall find him at home?'

'Not just now. They're all out—Mrs. Josselin can't rest. They've gone to send some more telegrams since seeing me. You see I should have told them before, but I didn't like to show the letter, for fear Sheila should be angry. And I never thought of the gypsies till this morning, when I couldn't stand it any more, and I told mother about the letter and she sent me over at once. She's ill or she'd have come herself.'

One word had caught Mr. Flower's ear specially.

'About the gypsies,' he said. 'How do you know about them, my boy?'

Then Conan told him all he knew—how he had met old Diana the day of the birthday party, just before he found Sheila and Mildred, and that it had struck him afterwards that they looked rather 'queer' when he mentioned her—about the letter too, sent to him for Sheila by Mildred Frost, which he had felt at such a loss about after hearing of his young friend's disappearance.

'I wish now I'd told of it sooner,' he said.

Then he looked up wistfully into the stranger's face.

'Won't you tell me who you are and why Sheila went to *you?*' he said. *I've* told you all I can.'

During this time they had been walking towards the wood. Mr. Flower hesitated.

'I think I must have a talk with Mr. Josselin first,' he said. 'But you have trusted me, so you deserve something in return. This much I can tell you. I am Sheila's uncle, her mother's brother.'

Conan opened his eyes in amazement.

'Mrs. Josselin's brother,' he said, and George could not help smiling a little.

'You will understand all about it afterwards,' he said. 'I am not very like Mrs. Josselin, am I?'

'No,' said Con, with a boy's frankness, 'I can't say you are. But Sheila's the very image of her mother—dark hair and eyes—and Honor's as fair as anything. So likenesses don't count for much, you see.'

'Honor?' Mr. Flower repeated, with a questioning in his voice. 'Let me see; Honor is Sheila's second name. Is—oh yes, I think Sheila mentioned it as—as the younger girl's name too.'

'It isn't *Sheila's* name,' said Conan. 'I know it isn't, for I wrote her name in full in the birthday book I gave her at Christmas. Sheila's second name is Margaret.'

A curious sensation came over Mr. Flower, a feeling as if he were on the verge of something that would throw new light on the whole position of things.

'Can I have been mistaken?' he said to himself; 'can that child have been deceiving me for some extraordinary reason?'

But this second thought he put away almost before it took shape in his mind.

'No, no, she was quite in earnest, poor girl, but——'

Just yet, however, he felt it better to say no more to his young companion.

'Have you any idea,' he asked Conan, 'how soon Mr. Josselin is likely to be back?'

'He won't be very long,' said the boy. 'They

keep hoping for a telegram or something all day, so they'll soon come in. Every time I think they hope they'll find Sheila herself,' and the boy smiled rather ruefully. 'But they are happier since I brought the letter and told them all I knew. Mr. Josselin said he began to see daylight through it at last. And now *you* can tell them that she's safe at your house it'll be all right again.'

'I hope so. I hope so indeed,' said Mr. Flower, though his own mind was bewildered and perplexed still.

'There's something I don't understand about it,' Con went on. 'It's not curiosity, it isn't really, that makes me ask you. It's just that I'm so very fond of Sheila. Honor's a dear little thing, and I like her still better for being so unhappy about Sheila, but Sheila's always been so kind to me.'

Mr. Flower looked at him with sympathy.

'I cannot tell you any more at present, my dear boy,' he said. 'If you like to wait till I have seen Mr. Josselin——' but Con shook his head.

'No, thank you, I can't. I must go home, for mother is anxious too. I *am* glad I can tell her that Sheila's safe, anyway. I'll come over again this evening or to-morrow.'

'Yes, do,' said the stranger, and then they shook hands heartily, and Con turned to make his way towards home, through the wood again; while Mr. Flower walked on to the front of the house by a path among the shrubberies which the boy pointed out to him.

In reply to his inquiry for Mr. Josselin, the footman who opened the door told him what he had expected to hear—that his master was out, but would probably return before long, and when Mr. Flower said he would wait till Mr. Josselin came in, the man eyed him doubtfully.

'My master is in great trouble just now, sir,' he began, hesitating a little over the last word; 'but——'

An older servant in plain clothes came forward. He had more perception than the footman, and, as he afterwards announced in the servants' hall, 'liked the look' of the stranger.

'Excuse me, sir,' he said respectfully, 'is it perhaps—have you possibly brought news of our young lady?'

'Yes,' said Mr. Flower, 'I have, good news, that is why I am anxious to see your master as soon as possible.'

Then all was eagerness and cordiality, for the butler was an old servant, much attached to Mr. and Mrs. Josselin, even though Sheila's temper had not endeared her personally to those about her. And Mr. Flower was shown into the library and offered refreshments, while Pender hung about, evidently dying to hear more.

But the stranger stood silently by the window, gazing out at the fair prospect before him, and trying to explain the contradictions still perplexing him.

Scarcely half an hour had passed when a carriage drove up rapidly. Then a colloquy in the hall ensued, followed by a rush of eager steps towards the library, the door of which was thrown open and three people hurried in. A sweet-faced woman with dark hair, and eyes swollen and painful from many tears, a man scarcely less agitated, and a little girl, the first glance at whose face sent a strange thrill through George Flower.

'Oh! have you brought us news of Sheila? Have you found her? Oh! it is not a mistake, is it?' were the questions and exclamations that came showering upon him.

And the farmer's ruddy face grew pale and his eyes seemed misty, as he hastened to answer, laying his hand gently on the golden-haired child who, in her eagerness, had caught hold of his rough tweed coat.

'No, no! it is no mistake. Sheila is safe at home with—with my mother and my wife. But'—and his hand clasped little Honor more closely—'I—I think there *has* been a mistake, nevertheless.'

For his agitation did not *all* arise from sympathy with the distressed family.

CHAPTER XII

CHRISTMAS GUESTS

SHEILA, as 'Aunt Mary' had prophesied, was quite well again in a day or two. And when she came downstairs to join in the family life of the farm, she found Mr. George Flower there in his usual place. It did not strike her that he had been away.

That first day and some following ones she hung about doing nothing in particular, for it seemed to her that she had nothing to do. Bessie and her mother were as busy as they could be; even granny saw to her poultry and her garden, and, old as she was, never thought of sitting down quietly to her knitting till after the early dinner was over and the dishes and plates nicely 'tidied away.' The Flowers kept one servant, a clean, rough country girl, but they superintended and directed everything themselves—Mrs. George Flower and her daughter, indeed, working harder than Sheila had ever seen any of the maids do at Curlew Moor.

'I can't stay here long,' she said to herself. 'To begin with, I don't want to live upon them. I can never feel as if they were really relations. And I should *never* get used to such a life. I must speak to—to Mr. George Flower about trying to get some sort of situation in a school,' and she determined to do so that very evening.

But she did not need to seek for an opportunity. George Flower had been watching her, pitying her, and yet seeing her faults more and more clearly.

'You are not happy with us, Sheila,' he said, coming into the kitchen, where, as she thought by chance, she was sitting alone. 'I'm afraid our plain ways don't suit you. But then we must remember you were not happy at Curlew either; you had so much to bear there.'

A sob rose into Sheila's throat.

'No, no!' she said, 'I don't think that *now*. I think the only real reason of my unhappiness was my own temper. I told you so the other day, Mr. Flower—you are not quite fair upon me.'

'Why don't you call me "Uncle George"?' he said.

Sheila grew red.

'I—I don't know,' she replied. 'You've all been very good to me, but—somehow I can't feel as if I really belonged to you. I'm afraid there's something about me that makes it impossible for any one to love me. You must see that *they* don't—if they had, they would never have let all this time pass without trying to find me.'

'How do you know they have not?' said the farmer, his usual kind voice sounding almost severe. 'You are very childish, Sheila. Surely you must know that even if—Mr. and Mrs. Josselin were glad to be rid of you, they are honourable and sensible people. Of course they have made every possible search for you—you were in their charge.'

Sheila's heart sank, if possible, lower.

'Then do they know where I am?' she said faintly.

'Yes.'

'But they haven't written to me.'

'Could you expect it? Did you consider them or their feelings when you left your home secretly?'

'No,' more faintly still. Then, in a moment or two: 'Then they have quite thrown me off?' with another choked sob. 'And—what do you want me to do? It is true I am not happy here. I am miserable, and only a burden. I—I think dear granny loves me a little, but none of the rest of you do, or can. I would like to get something to do. I could be a sort of under-teacher in a school, I think.'

'Anything of that kind is out of the question at present,' said Mr. Flower. 'You must remember that Mr. Josselin is your legal guardian. Both you and—and little Honor are entirely in his charge——'

'Of course Honor is,' Sheila interrupted, 'she is his own daughter.'

'You are as much in his hands as she is,' resumed the farmer. 'I—I have communicated with him and Mrs. Josselin. They have decided that for the present you are to stay here. You have caused them intense anxiety. Indeed, I wonder it did not make Mrs. Josselin seriously ill—she has suffered terribly, I believe.'

The sob was not to be choked down this time. Sheila burst into an agony of tears.

'Mamma, O dear, dear mamma!' she cried. 'And—oh, to think she is *not* mamma!'

Mr. George Flower turned away, and for a moment or two he did not speak. Then he said, and his tone was now gentler and more sympathising—

'You do love her, my poor child, I see, and indeed they all deserve your love. Well, then, try to cheer up a little. Show them you want to please them—to make what amends you can.'

'How can I?' she said, looking up, her dark eyes streaming with tears.

'Submit unrepiningly to what they wish you to do. Try to make use of your time. There are many things Bessie and her mother can teach you which you will all your life be the better for knowing. Begin to-morrow morning.˙ Get up when my girl does, early—you are quite well now—and go the round of her work with her, helping all you can. Then granny would like nothing better than to teach you knitting, when the quiet time of the day comes on. Think how proud your—Mr. Josselin would be of a pair of socks of your own making as a Christmas present.'

'Do you think he would—really? Do you think they can ever forgive me—that perhaps, some day, if I try very, very hard to improve, they would trust me to be with darling Honor again, and ask me to pay them a little visit? Though—oh, I *don't* know if I could bear it?' and the tears rushed back again.

George Flower laid his hand on the bowed head.

'My dear,' he said, almost solemnly, 'leave the future. Clouds disperse in ways we cannot foresee in the least. Do your best in the present from now, and never give up hope.'

'I suppose you mean that—that one gets accustomed to things that seem at first unendurable,' said Sheila gently. 'Well—I will try—some day it *may* seem different, if—if only they ever forgive me. You are very kind and I do thank you. I would like to do something to please you yourself, if I could.'

The good man smiled. He felt very much encouraged.

'Will you do this for me?' he said. 'In the evenings, can you give my Bessie a little teaching? She has had less than she should have had, poor child, being needed at home to help her mother. And she is not a stupid girl.'

'No, I'm sure she isn't,' said Sheila heartily. 'Yes, if she won't mind, I'd like very much to teach her anything I'm further on in than she is. If you're sure she won't mind?'

Bessie 'mind'! No, she was far too simple and sensible, and the evening hours over their books drew the two girls nearer together in many ways. And despite some sad hours, and terrible fits of homesickness and remorse, Sheila kept her promise. She tried her best to be cheerful and useful and good-tempered, and when she failed—for habit is a formidable enemy as well as a useful friend—she did not, thanks in great measure to the kindness of those about her, and granny's good advice, lose heart too entirely. The struggle was hard, but Sheila was brave, and she felt that her efforts were noted, and that 'some day' the dear ones who she felt would always be her *dearest* might know how strong a motive with her had been the wish to please them.

Three months from the day of her arrival at Moorecroft you would scarcely have known Sheila Josselin for the same girl. She had grown stronger in reality and in appearance; there was even a tinge of colour in her pale face. Her eyes now looked one brightly in the face, her forehead was scarcely ever puckered up into its old peevish wrinkles, and though the prevailing expression of the delicate features was perhaps melancholy, it was at the same time sweet and gentle; the bitter captiousness was gone.

She had grown used to the plain and homely ways of her new friends, and had learnt to value the rare honesty of character, the cheerful unselfishness under

Mrs. George Flower's rather rough and bustling manner. And in many little things she had been of use to her new friends, which they were the first to recognise. There was a certain daintiness about the table; prettily arranged nosegays of flowers, or leaves when the flowers were over, stood about here and there on the old-fashioned window sill; there were white muslin blinds tied back with red ribbon—ever so many small additions which delighted Bessie, and made her declare that Sheila's fingers were like a fairy's.

'The place has quite a different look now. I can't think why mother and I never thought of all these nice fancies,' she would say admiringly, and very proud she felt of herself a week or two before Christmas, when her new dark-blue serge dress, which had been made and fitted under Sheila's directions, came home from the small neighbouring town where the Flowers did their shopping.

Sheila smiled at her pleasure. But when Bessie had run off, she could not smother the sigh which *would* come.

Last Christmas—oh, to think of the difference! And what a horrid temper she had been in all day about some ridiculously trifling cause of offence.

And how dear, loving little Honor had hung over her, trying to coax her into good-humour again, and how patient Miss Burke had been, and—and—— No—she just *must* not think of it all.

There was a good deal of excitement and bustle at the farm in preparation for Christmas, much more than had ever been the case before, though this Sheila did not know, and Bessie had been warned to let her take it as a matter of course.

'We are expecting friends—one relation and two friends,' Mrs. George Flower told her, when the spare bedrooms which, as Sheila knew, were sometimes used by visitors in the summer came to be overhauled.

Cleaner than they were they could scarcely be, but great fires were lighted, in front of which the mattresses and blankets were thoroughly 'aired,' and some of old Mrs. Flower's *very* best linen—the homespun Buckinghamshire sheets and pillow-cases which granny was so proud of, and which had been carefully stored in England all the years she had been in America—were taken out of the 'napery press,' in honour of the expected guests. And Bessie and her mother anxiously consulted her as to many little matters on which they felt her experience was much greater than theirs.

It was Sheila's fingers that made the pretty pin-cushions for both rooms, and nailed up the neat little muslin blinds behind the washhandstands; Sheila who arranged the winter posies—for there is always *something* of which one can make a posy in the country—of ivy and bright berries and tinted leaves on the dressing-tables, the evening before the day on which the visitors were expected.

'Don't the rooms look cosy now?' she said to Bessie, when the last touches had been given. 'Those new strips of crimson druggeting look *so* nice beside the white dimity.'

'Yes, indeed, and to think how little they cost. That was all your idea, Sheila,' said Bessie.

'I wish I knew something about your friends. Which of them is a relation? The old lady or the young one?'

'Neither is an old lady,' said Bessie. 'But you'd best ask mother. I've never seen them. It's not the same ladies that come in the summer.'

And as at that moment Mrs. Flower was heard calling Sheila to ask her to decorate the home-made Christmas cake and dishes of apples and pears which were to appear as dessert with some of her pretty leaves, the girl ran downstairs, and while at work repeated her inquiry. But Aunt Mary was not much more communicative than Bessie. She'd never seen these friends of her husband's either, but he thought a great deal of them, and she was sure they'd be very pleasant and friendly.

Still Sheila could not help wishing they were not coming. It made her feel still sadder and lonelier to be helping in preparations for ' a merry Christmas' in which she could take no real share. But then she checked herself. This was selfish—and selfishness she now knew had been her great enemy. So she tried to look cheerful and interested, though, as the hour approached at which the guests were expected, she asked Aunt Mary if she might go round to the church again, to finish some of the Christmas dressing which she and Bessie had helped with.

'You'll not be long, then, my dear. Not more than an hour. I may want you to help with the tea,' for one of Sheila's suggestions had been that tea, neatly set out on a small table in the best parlour, which was of course to be used at this festive time, would be a very welcome sight to the travellers.

She gave Mrs. George Flower the required promise, and within the time named her slight figure, in its warm 'Mother Hubbard' cloak, might have been seen making its way home across the frosty fields. She was wondering if *perhaps* Christmas would bring her an answer to the long letter expressing humble and heartfelt sorrow for the past which, with Mr. George Flower's permission, she had sent a week or two ago to Mr. and Mrs. Josselin. It had been terribly hard to write—not from any remains of false pride, but because it was such anguish not to be able to address them as her father and mother. And she had ended after all by saying—

'I *cannot* write anything but dearest papa and mamma,' and by signing herself, 'Your own Sheila.'

There was no sign of bustle about the farmhouse as she came up to the door, the fact being that the guests had arrived very soon after she went out. But Sheila thought to herself that they could not yet have come, and she opened the best parlour door, meaning to see if all there was in order. Some one had been watching for her, though she did not know it, and as she entered the room, George Flower quietly made his way out by the other door leading into the kitchen, leaving the three newcomers by themselves.

Sheila started as she saw the figures dark against the windows.—P. 195.

Sheila started as she saw the figures dark against the windows.

'They have come,' was her first thought. Then 'O mamma — O papa — O Onnie!' and with a great gasp she staggered back, almost falling on the floor.

They were all round her at once—all their arms seemed to be encircling her, all the three dear, dear faces, with smiles contradicting the tears that would come, seemed pressed together to hers. But then came the sorrowful afterthought—

'No, no—forgive me. I mustn't say papa and mamma,' and a flood of anguish rushed in upon her joy.

'My darling—our darling—yes, yes, you may. It is true—you *are* our Sheila.'

And then they told her all—little Honor standing by, bright-faced and happy, though Sheila's first thought was of intense sympathy for *her*.

No ; Honor did not want sympathy of that kind. The knowledge that *she*, not Sheila, was the orphan child of Godfrey and Lettice Josselin, had come to her at the same moment as the news of Sheila's safety. Both had been the result of Mr. George Flower's visit to Curlew Moor, the morning he met

Conan Sherwood. And the joy had conquered the grief, if indeed so sunny and unselfish a nature as Honor's could have felt real grief at anything which would make another, and that other her dear 'sister,' happy.

'I don't mind, darling,' she whispered. 'They love me just as much, and I'm always to be their own little girl too. I liked to feel as if I were giving up something to you.'

It took some time to explain all—the reason of the secrecy which Mrs. Josselin had so dreaded—and which, now that the single-minded goodness and disinterestedness of the Flowers were evident, had been proved to be so uncalled for. And Sheila herself was the first to say that the lesson she had learnt had been in no way too severe.

'We could scarcely bear to do it,' said her mother; 'to leave you all these weeks under the mistake. But——'

'It was my own doing, mamma. *Nothing* could have taught me as well. And *oh*, the joy of it now! Can I ever be thankful enough?'

There were other happy and thankful hearts too at Moorecroft that Christmas. The good Flowers had learnt to love Sheila, and she to love them; but still, the moment they saw golden-haired Honor they felt that *she* was their 'Lettice's baby.' And though Honor was not yet quite the age at which her grandfather Josselin had agreed that she was to hear the truth, as it had come to her in the way it had, there was now nothing to prevent her spending some part of her holidays every year with her mother's family.

Sheila often came with her, and the Moorecroft relations were always Granny and Uncle and Aunt to her.

'It makes us seem still *realer* sisters,' Honor often said.

Honor found an unexpected Christmas present on her dressing-table the next morning. It was the unfortunate 'sachet,' which Sheila had brought away in her bundle, and which, in spite of one or two marks which she could not *quite* remove, she had never had the heart to throw away.

As time went on, Honor was able to be of great use to her good relations, who had not even known the fact of her being heir to Joyce Court and her grandfather's wealth. She grew up to be one of the few women whose natures remain unspoilt by such a position—simple, unselfish, and faithful.

Poor old Diana never knew of her mistake. Not many months after the happy Christmas I have told you of, one of her 'boys' brought news to Moorecroft of her death, which he said had been peaceful and untroubled.

'And she bid me say as she prayed for a blessing on them whose goodness to her she'd never forgot,' added the dark-eyed messenger.

THE END

Printed by R. & R. CLARK, *Edinburgh.*

By Mrs. MOLESWORTH.

MY NEW HOME. By Mrs. MOLESWORTH. Illustrated by LESLIE BROOKE. Crown 8vo. 4s. 6d.

MARY. By Mrs. MOLESWORTH. With Illustrations by LESLIE BROOKE. Crown 8vo. 4s. 6d.

Also Illustrated by LESLIE BROOKE. Globe 8vo. 2s. 6d. each.

    NURSE HEATHERDALE'S STORY.
    THE GIRLS AND I.

Illustrated by WALTER CRANE. Globe 8vo. 2s. 6d. each.

    A CHRISTMAS POSY.
    'CARROTS,' JUST A LITTLE BOY.
    A CHRISTMAS CHILD.
    CHRISTMAS-TREE LAND.
    THE CUCKOO CLOCK.
    FOUR WINDS FARM.
    GRANDMOTHER DEAR.
    HERR BABY.
    LITTLE MISS PEGGY.
    THE RECTORY CHILDREN.
    ROSY.
    THE TAPESTRY ROOM.
    TELL ME A STORY.
    TWO LITTLE WAIFS.
    'US': AN OLD-FASHIONED STORY.
    CHILDREN OF THE CASTLE.

By Miss ROSSETTI.

GOBLIN MARKET. By CHRISTINA G. ROSSETTI. With 18 Page Illustrations and other Decorations by LAURENCE HOUSMAN. Cloth, elegant. 5s.

SING-SONG: A NURSERY RHYME BOOK. By CHRISTINA G. ROSSETTI. With 120 Illustrations by ARTHUR HUGHES, engraved by the Brothers Dalziel. Small 4to. 4s. 6d.

MACMILLAN AND CO., LONDON.

BOOKS FOR YOUNG READERS.

Globe 8vo. Cloth extra. 2s. 6d. each.

OUR YEAR. By Mrs. CRAIK.

LITTLE SUNSHINE'S HOLIDAY. By Mrs. CRAIK.

WHEN I WAS A LITTLE GIRL. By the Author of 'St. Olave's.'

NINE YEARS OLD. By the Author of 'When I was a Little Girl,' etc.

A STOREHOUSE OF STORIES. Edited by C. M. YONGE. Two Vols.

AGNES HOPETOUN'S SCHOOLS AND HOLIDAYS. By Mrs. OLIPHANT.

THE STORY OF A FELLOW-SOLDIER. By FRANCES AWDRY. (A Life of Bishop Patteson for the Young.)

RUTH AND HER FRIENDS : A Story for Girls.

THE HEROES OF ASGARD : Tales from Scandinavian Mythology. By A. and E. KEARY.

THE RUNAWAY. By the Author of 'Mrs. Jerningham's Journal.'

WANDERING WILLIE. By the Author of 'Conrad the Squirrel.'

PANSIE'S FLOUR BIN. Illustrated by ADRIAN STOKES.

MILLY AND OLLY. By Mrs. T. H. WARD. Illustrated.

THE POPULATION OF AN OLD PEAR TREE : Or, Stories of Insect Life. From the French of E. VAN BRUYSSEL. Edited by C. M. YONGE. Illustrated.

HANNAH TARNE. By MARY E. HULLAH. Illustrated by W. J. HENNESSY.

MACMILLAN AND CO., LONDON.

CPSIA information can be obtained
at www.ICGtesting.com
Printed in the USA
LVHW021218030523
745890LV00010B/560